Baseballs Don't Bounce

My Journey From Hopelessness to Happiness... and The Three Words That Changed My Life

Forrest Willett

ISBN-13: 978-1511677394

ISBN-10: 1511677392

This book is dedicated to my wife Julie,
who did not give up on me
and believed in me when
I did not believe in myself.
To my son and best friend
Hunter, who taught me that
baseballs don't bounce.
I thank you both for accepting
me for who I am.
And to my mother Patricia,
although I have never known you,
I love you and forgive you.

Table of Contents

Foreword

Forrest Willett is one of the most inspiring, loving and beautiful human beings I have ever met.

It turns out Forrest ran across me several years before I ran across him. He was lying in bed, physically incapacitated, physically and emotionally depressed as the result of a severe traumatic brain injury due to an automobile accident. Forrest heard me on television promoting my book, *The Success Principles*. After he heard me talking about how the book could help anyone, even people in Forrest's condition, get from where they were to where they wanted to be, he got a copy of my book. As difficult as it was to read with his traumatized brain, he slowly struggled through it page by page. As he began to apply the principles, his life began to dramatically change.

The story of Forrest's transformation is incredibly moving and inspiring ... so much so that I opened the 10th Anniversary revised edition of *The Success Principles* with the story of how Forrest overcame his huge challenges and went on to become a powerful motivational speaker and transformational trainer.

Over the past six years Forrest has taken many of my trainings, has become a Canfield Success Principles Trainer and, most importantly, has become a close personal friend and colleague. He is one of the most loving, funny and inspirational people I know. His passion and enthusiasm for life are contagious. His compassion for others and his commitment to making a difference are palpable.

Whenever he speaks, magic happens. Hearts are opened, dreams are rekindled, negative beliefs are replaced with positive expectations, fear is replaced with courage and conviction, and his students go on to achieve what they never before thought was possible.

In this wonderful and readable book, Forrest shares his journey from hopelessness to happiness and reveals the principles he used to reclaim his life when all the experts told him he couldn't do it.

Whether you are faced with a seemingly impossible challenge like Forrest's, or you just want to achieve a little more love, joy and success in your life, this book will inspire you and help guide you to do it.

Whatever it is that might be holding you back in life, the stories and action steps in this book will help you believe in yourself, transform your thoughts, discover what you truly want and go about getting it.

Enjoy reading this book and putting its valuable principles into action.

— **Jack Canfield**, Coauthor of *The Success Principles™* and the *Chicken Soup for the Soul®* series.

Chapter One

The Day my Whole World Stopped

October 6, 2002, I lost the most important person in my life in a horrific car wreck. It was not my wife or my son, I lost myself. Yes, I am the man who lost himself. I lost who I was as a husband, father and friend. I lost my ability to read, write and speak fluently. I was a two-year-old child in a 31-year-old body, everything around me was new and extremely frustrating. I could not even control my balance while walking, I looked like a baby deer on a frozen pond trying to stand up straight. Early on this would cause me to fall down a flight of stairs, breaking my leg and landing me in a wheelchair once again. I often wondered what went wrong, why did this happen? Just weeks before the accident, I was a successful entrepreneur with offices in eight cities and 23 employees. Now I was couldn't even count change to buy a coffee.

At the time of the accident I had my car for sale and a gentlemen wanted to take it for a test drive. I gave him the keys and sat in the passenger seat. That's all I remember. Later through the police investigation it was revealed that the driver was speaking on his cell phone with his son and lost control of the vehicle at a high rate of speed. The accident scene was one of confusion because even though the car came back as registered to myself, the police and members of the fire department knew that it wasn't me driving the car. I was a volunteer fire fighter for 10 years and personally knew everyone on that department. They knew I did not have a moustache or glasses and the person in the passenger seat was unrecognizably swollen, bloody and unconscious with no identification.

My left arm was flopping around and broken in several places. I can't believe how devastated they must have been to see me in this unrecognizable condition. Even my good friend who was a paramedic at the scene later said he could not believe it was me. Yet just hours before I had been at the fire captain's house visiting with my son and feeling on top of the world.

My first memories were 10 days later waking up in the hospital. They were very foggy memories as I slipped in and out of consciousness. The only thing that felt familiar was the constant ringing in my ears and the sound of the blood pressure monitors "beep beep beep". My first thought was, "What happened to my arm?" because I could not move it, and "Why is my mouth full of stitches inside and out?" My wife Julie walked into the hospital room with my then two-year-old son Hunter. Although I recognized them, I was frustrated that I didn't remember their names. As a matter of fact I didn't remember the names of many people in my life. If you have ever known anyone with Alzheimer's disease, then you know that losing your memory is one of the most devastating things in life and here I was 31 years old and mine was gone.

All it took was one split second and our lives were changed forever. We were both left with traumatic brain injuries. Through later testing with the Glasgow Outcome Scale, I was declared to have a catastrophic brain injury. The results stated that I had a permanent loss of 55 percent or more of myself, both mentally and emotionally.

How lucky can one person be? Very few people are given a second chance in life, and I was grateful to be given a third chance. Yes a third, you see this was my second traumatic brain injury. The first occurred when I was two and fell down the basement stairs and suffered a sub-dural hematoma, which required surgical intervention to relieve the pressure from my brain. I have been reminded of this injury and how lucky I am everyday as I wash my hair and run my hand over the area where the bone was removed.

Everything in life had changed. Friends would drop by to visit and tell Julie and I about their weekend of boating at the cottage. When they asked what we had been up to, Julie would share the events of our week, "Forrest learned to brush his teeth and shave on his own and he did not cut his face once, I'm so proud of him. And next week he will be working with his speech therapist on a grocery list and if he's feeling up to it he may actually go to the grocery store and try to complete the list with his occupational therapist if his anxiety does not stop him at the door." As friends and visitors would come to the house, they could not help but notice large laminated signs on the fridge, stove and doors. They were reminders for me not to touch the stove, to remember to put things back into the fridge and to contact someone before I went outside. We also had another person in the house, a rehabilitation support worker, who I called my babysitter. On the advice of my support team, I needed to have 24-hour attentive care to keep me safe from my own actions. Many people have experienced the frustration of coming out of the mall and forgetting where they've parked their car. I would walk just a few blocks and forget where my house was. We were very fortunate to live in a small community where everyone knew everybody so when I lost my sense of direction our neighbors would kindly help me get back home. This must have been unbelievably difficult for Julie and I don't know why she stayed with me, but I am grateful that she did. She herself has transformed from a go-getter to a go-giver.

I had a whole team of professionals working with me daily. Some of them where neurologists, psychologists, psychiatrists, surgeons, physiotherapists, speech language pathologists, occupational therapists and the list goes on and on. Close your eyes for a minute and just imagine if you had a dozen or more of the top professionals in their field whose full-time job was to help you get from where you are to where you want to be. Even though they are working with you tirelessly day after day, year after year, the progress is incredibly slow and unfortunately you're not reaching your ultimate goal. How would you feel?

I began to spiral faster and faster into a deep pit of depression. Anger and despair and the feeling of hopelessness and helplessness became the flavor of the day. My favorite activity became lying in bed all day in between my therapy sessions. I also became dependent on prescription medication, anti-anxiety pills, sleeping pills, painkillers such as OxyContin and anti-depressants. At the time, I didn't realize how habit forming the pain relievers would become, just to get through the day. Years later I now see that the pain relieving effects of these drugs also soothes the pain of a broken heart and broken dreams. Not being able to see a better future can get people hooked on these drugs by chemically removing all of their fear and anxiety.

This was a letter written by my family doctor to the treatment team one and a half years post-accident.

"I have known Mr. Willett for over 20 years and I have watched him grow from a young boy into a very successful business person. As you know, he had a major motor vehicle accident October 6, 2002 at which time Mr. Willett was a passenger in the car that was involved in a single vehicle rollover. He suffered a major traumatic brain injury at the time and was unconscious at the scene, had facial trauma that knocked out several teeth and fractured left humerus. At the present time, he presents as a pleasant handsome gentleman who is able to carry on a superficial conversation. However, I have major concerns regarding Mr. Willett and that he has trouble with his attention span and cannot hold onto thoughts for a sustained period of time. He has certainly lost a substantial part of his judgment and his ability to speak fluently has been substantially reduced from what it was.

My understanding of the notes from the speech and language pathology assessment is that he has major problems with reading comprehension and short-term verbal memory. This is well documented in the literature. This gentleman, certainly at present, is unable to function in his job as an entrepreneur at the head of a fairly large and complex company. He certainly does not show the wit and depth of thinking that he had prior to the injury. It is my opinion that he will never be able to go back to the level of work he was doing prior to the injury.

I have concerns that when something like this happens it often leads to breakups in families further down the road and major depression that will further impact on his ability to function as the person he once was.

It is strongly held in my opinion that this gentleman has a psychological and/or mental impairment that will affect his life; at least 55% or more his ability to function as a father, to make a living and enjoy life, has been changed." February 12, 2004

A year later, just two and a half years after the date of the accident, a neuropsychological assessment that spanned over four days of testing had concluded that I had plateaued, this means I had reached 95 to 98% of my spontaneous recovery and that I should not expect any further spontaneous recovery.

The doctor said I should feel lucky just to be alive, but I wasn't so sure about that. Two and a half years, that's all they give you? 912.5 days ... hope has to last longer than that.

This news was another blow to my recovery and diminishing self-esteem. I thought to myself, "How many times can a human being be beaten down and continue to get up?" With all of the diagnoses from the doctors it may look like I was a modern-day Frankenstein. Catastrophic brain injury, clinical depression, several anxiety disorders, post-traumatic stress disorder, mild aphasia and I could go on. I had many thoughts of what's the use, why even try anymore. I could not get excited about anything for the fear of failure was ever looming. I was a real mess. The days and months went up and down between hope, suicidal thoughts and grey numbness in between. I had no emotions and no control over my own life other than breathing and eating. I felt like a puppet on a string being toted around by well-meaning doctors and therapists. Like a timid little puppy afraid of getting into trouble, I did just as they said, although I felt as if I was getting nowhere. Everything changed when my favorite hobby of lying in bed finally paid off big-time one morning. I felt as if I had hit the jackpot!

"Human Kind. Be both." — Forrest Willett

Chapter Two

The Day My World Started Again

We all have days in our lives that we will never forget. Something so significant happens that you remember the exact time and place you were such as the day JFK was shot or the day the twin towers fell in New York on 9/11. You remember where you were, who you were with, and sometimes even what you were wearing.

My significant day came as I was lying in bed with the blankets pulled over my head, waiting for the world to go away. I heard the morning show host on television say, "Coming up next is Jack Canfield with his new book, *the Success Principles*, how to get from where you are to where you want to be." In my head I thought this is probably more crap, until the commercial was over and they introduced Jack. He claimed that his new book could help anyone get from where they are to where they want to be. He went on to say that your current circumstances and past situations didn't matter. You can transform your life by applying these principles.

For the first time in years, I sat up and pulled the covers off my head. I clearly remember the words Jack said, "If you could do anything in life and there were no limitations, what would you do?"

I remember chuckling to myself and saying if I could do anything in life and there were no limitations, "I would take my three biggest disabilities and turn them into assets. Not only would I learn to read and write, I would become a #1 best-selling author, and not only would I learn to speak fluently again, I would become a professional speaker and not only would I beat depression, I would inspire others to do the same."

I chuckled again thinking, "Yeah right" and asked my wife to write down the man's name because I wanted to buy his book.

Julie looked at me confused and said, "You can't even read your son a bedtime story, how are you going to read such a book"? Julie does not sugar coat anything. I exclaimed, "Yes but this man said that if I do this, this and this, I can transform my life."

Julie entertained me and brought me to the bookstore for one reason, she said she had not seen me that excited about anything in years. I finally had that spark back in my eyes ... that was until I presented the book to my speech therapist and told her of my plan.

I was nervous of her reaction because at the time I always expected the worst and braced myself for the fact she may not be supportive of such a large undertaking.

My speech therapist was very supportive as always, especially since this was the first time she had seen me this excited about my recovery. She explained a few roadblocks I may run into. First, I could not read very well or comprehend what I was reading. At that time I was just learning to read a children's book to my son.

The second roadblock was the immense size of this book, over 450 pages. The children books I was reading at the time where 8 to 12 pages and it would take me multiple readings to comprehend them. When reading a book to my son at night, he would often say "That's not what it says daddy".

You see, my wife would read the same book to him every night, and he knew the words in the order they were to come. He would spend no time letting me know when I had made a mistake. This would bring up a series of considerations, fears and roadblocks in my own head. Seriously, how could I write a book when I have not yet re-learned the basics of spelling?

And the thought of being a professional speaker made me nervous to say the least. On the rare occasion we went out for breakfast, I would just ask Julie to read the menu and I would order OOrange J J J J J J J J J Juice.

Whenever my anxiety would arise, my stuttering went out of control and the thought of speaking in front of people brought on anxiety. Kids are honest and sometimes the truth hurts. I remember one of Hunters' friends saying, "Your dad talks funny," and his reply was, "That's how he talks".

I was determined to read *The Success Principles* and change my life. I knew where I wanted to be, I just did not know how to get there. My speech therapist and I made an agreement that I would give myself one year to read the book and if it was too difficult, I would not beat myself up emotionally as I had done in the past.

I was now motivated more than ever not only to learn how to read and comprehend, but to show everyone that there is life after a brain injury and depression.

Christine, my speech therapist, created many strategies for me to read the book, such as highlighting, underlining and using a white envelope to slide down the lines one at a time so I would not skip lines and get confused.

Over the next week I did a really big life review, going over areas in my life where I had not taken 100% responsibility and there were many.

I first started to take responsibility with my family and then my rehabilitation. I had been lying in bed all day waiting for the therapists to show up and "make" me better, not realizing that I had to do the work, especially when they were gone. Jim Rohn says, "You can't hire other people to do your push-ups". It now made total sense that I had to take complete responsibility in order for me to get better. Even though my family and therapists were there to assist me, I was the one in the end that was responsible for doing the work.

We are all self-made people, yet it is usually the successful people who will admit it. It took a lot for me to admit to myself that I had created the life I was living. It was time for me to get down to work and escape this self-created prison I was living in. It was time to "Take action."

I soon started to apply the success principles from Jack's book into all areas of my life. To my amazement, life started to become easier, as I was able to release the brakes and accept life as it unfolded. I stopped trying to be who I wasn't and be myself. Life was very difficult trying to put on a fake smile and pretend to be something I wasn't. I just wanted to be me and accept who I was and where I was at this point in my life. When I did, things began to change for the better.

"Take action" is a principle that has allowed me to make massive changes in my life. As I was recovering in what seemed like leaps and bounds, I was asked by many organizations to share my story. For quite awhile I turned them down, until the day I decided to take action.

The March of Dimes is an organization that helps many people with physical and mental disabilities. They were having their annual conference and asked me if I could share my story of success and triumph over adversity. Although I agreed, I thought in my head, "Oh my God, what have I gotten myself into, I am not a professional speaker." And I only had 10 days to prepare.

It was time for me to "Act as if." This was my big chance to reach one of my biggest goals in life and I wasn't about to let it slip through my fingers. I prepared a speech with the help of my speech therapist and read it over and over again for several days. On the day of the speech, I walked into the convention center and saw a room of 287 people. This was the first time in over a year that I wish I still had an anti-anxiety pill!

Sweat rolled down my back like an April rain shower. When I stood up at the podium, my hands were shaking so bad that I could not read the paper. So I set the paper down, took a deep breath and said to myself, "This is it, I am finally here."

I looked around the room and started with a joke. I told the crowd that I was shaking so badly that I could thread a sewing machine while it was running. Their laughter put me at ease and I was able to share my story without the paper.

For the first time in my life, I received a standing ovation, and it gave me a rush of feelings that I cannot explain. After the talk was over, I was approached by several people who wanted me to speak at their organization. I was on cloud nine. Just a few short years ago I could not speak fluently or put a full sentence together that made much sense, and now people wanted to hire and pay me to speak ... wow.

In my commitment to constant and never ending improvement, I decided to get some training to be a professional speaker. The following February, I started on my journey with Jack Canfield as my personal mentor in his 'Train the Trainer' course.

And just like anything in life, along came the fears, considerations and roadblocks. On the first day of the course, I thought to myself, "What am I thinking? I'm not a professional speaker. What if all of these people I am surrounded by find out that I could not speak fluently just a few short years ago?"

I was given the opportunity to share my story on stage with all of these amazing people, and to my surprise, only good has come from that day forward. I have now been speaking in many different places all over the world such as India and Dubai. It is truly amazing, what can happen in life when you decide what you want, believe in yourself, set goals and take action.

The greatest transformation in my overall well-being came from applying three daily principles. Visualization, Practice persistence with patience and Practice the rule of five.

Through my recovery, one of my biggest obstacles was fatigue, the feeling of constantly being tired. This affects every aspect of your life, from relationships to your work life and your everyday well-being. My fatigue was caused from getting very little sleep at night, worrying about what the next day might bring. I was unable to slow down or turn off the negative thoughts going through my head.

I did three overnight sleep studies in the hospital and each time, the only result was a heavier prescription of sleeping pills.

I turned this around by making a list of my top five priority actions that I would do the following day towards my goals. I would then visualize the whole next day as if it were a movie playing in my head; the actions I would take and the activities I would do. It didn't happen overnight, but my sleep improved tremendously over the next few months. I did have a set back when I thought I had everything under control. I had begun to slack off on the visualization and rule of five, and fell back into my old sleeping patterns. It was then I realized that I had to practice persistence with patience if I wanted my positive changes to be long-term.

As my sleep improved, so did my relationship with my

wife and son and when that happened, I no longer felt as depressed. I went to my doctor with the goal of getting off the medication that I was told that I would likely be on for life. I exchanged the pills for exercise, diet and applying *The Success Principles*. I have been completely off all medication since August 2007, with no symptoms of depression or anxiety and I am still happily married.

After a lot of hard work and help from other people, I have exceeded my original goals. Not only can I speak fluently, read, and write, but I have also became a professional speaker and this is my second book on how to help people overcome depression. I now work with Jack Canfield, assisting with his trainings throughout the world. He has become a great friend and mentor. Jack has also shown me that dreams do come true when you follow them.

True transformation cannot occur with hope and willpower alone, we need specific tools to make lasting change. This book gives you the tools you need for that change; I am living proof of that. My transformation did not occur overnight. It took a long time, reaching one small goal after the other, which eventually turned into a massive change.

If I am able to overcome all of these obstacles in life and succeed at achieving my goals, imagine what is possible for you.

Building many houses in my life, I know that a solid foundation is the most important part of a solid home. If you don't have that, everything else will be out of alignment. When I hit rock bottom, I needed to start over and *The Success Principles* would be the solid foundation on which I would rebuild my life, and an extraordinary one at that.

My new speaking career began as I was attending support groups for people with an acquired brain injury, as well as volunteering in my community. I would meet people one-on-one who have an acquired brain injury and/or depression, and help them face their fears of the unknown and share my story with them. I found it very therapeutic for myself and for the people I am helping.

I strongly urge people to share their story, because by telling your story, the healing can start and you can let go of the emotional baggage that has been weighing you down.

The process of writing this book has been very challenging, given the fact that I had to relive all of the emotions I had struggled with for years. The good thing is, I now know how to handle those feelings and what they mean to me.

My son came home from school one day with the story of Humpty Dumpty, a popular children's story that reminds me of myself and others I have met. Many of us have had a great fall (brain injury and/or depression) and all the king's horses and all the king's men (Doctors and Therapists) couldn't put Humpty (You) back together again.

It all starts with you. YOU have to want to be put back together again and when you make that decision, of course you will need the help of doctors and therapists, family and friends. Just know they cannot put you back together on their own, you must work at it and fully participate in your own recovery.

"We search for mysteries at the far reaches of outer space, yet there are a great many strange and unknown things going on within the finite space of our own brains."
— Rich Maloof, Writer, Editor, and Musician

Please remember to pace yourself. If you try everything at once you will set yourself up for disappointment.

As the person who is struggling emotionally, we often see little, if any progress. I often compare the progress with the life of a puppy dog. If you bring home a new puppy and see it every day, you do not notice its growth. Yet if a friend stopped by once a month they would be astounded by the immense growth in such a short time. The same holds true for emotional growth—if we work on it every day, the people around you will notice the great changes in your life.

"You don't have to be a fantastic hero to do certain things; to complete. You can just be an ordinary person, sufficiently motivated to reach challenging goals. This intense effort, the giving of everything you've got, is a very pleasant bonus."
— Sir Edmund Hillary, Mountaineer

Chapter Three
Why I wanted to write this book

There are many good books written about acquired brain injury and depression by doctors and professionals. I found many of them very overwhelming, with language only a doctor can figure out or they were thicker than a phone book, which was overwhelming to look at too.

I wanted to write a book in plain, easy language that reads like butter and cuts like a knife, from someone who has gone through these dark times and transformed from tears to triumph. This is not a how-to book, but rather a how–to-think-about-things book. It is a book full of ideas, thoughts, and life lessons I have experienced on my journey overcoming a traumatic brain injury and depression.

Now that I have picked up the pieces and put myself back together again with the help of many people, it is my mission to help as many people as I can. That is what this book is all about. I have met so many people over the years who have felt the same way I did early on in my recovery; basically I felt hopeless, "Why try? This is useless," I would think to myself.

Dr. Davidson once told me about people with brain injuries who are studying to become doctors. I thought, "No way, this can't be, it just seems too unbelievable." Now that the clouds have cleared away, I can see clearly that what he told me was true. You can be, do and have whatever you want in life if you work at it.

I would like to share the same message with other people and pass on the things I have learned to triumph over a major adversity. Inspiring other people to find their own self-love, acceptance, and happiness now brings me a lot of joy.

If you have a brain injury or know someone with one, my

hope is that it can be detected early on. Studies have shown that early intervention is effective against many of its most damaging consequences, such as depression, anxiety, and ultimately alienation.

I will touch on subjects that may be embarrassing for some people to talk about. Let me share with you that the only way through these embarrassing or uncomfortable situations is to face them and talk about them, and once you can do that, they will no longer be uncomfortable or embarrassing.

This near death experience has given me a new perspective on life. When you are given a second or third chance you don't want to waste it. I am grateful to walk and speak and I no longer take things for granted. I treat everyone that I come into contact with the way I want to be treated, with kindness and unconditional love. I also treat myself the same way.

Ask yourself this question: If you talked to your friends the way you talk to yourself, would you have any friends left? Researchers tell us that we have approximately 50,000 thoughts a day go through our head and most of them are negative.

Just think back to this morning when you started your day. Did you beat yourself up emotionally? Most people do, and I used to as well. We say things like, "I'm overweight." "My hair looks like a mess and my butt looks fat in these jeans."

Now just imagine saying those same things to your best friend. You would never imagine doing that so why is it okay to talk to ourselves in that manner? It is time to stop the negative self-talk.

The great turnaround in my life came to me that day I

discovered baseballs don't bounce. As you will read later in the book, it was about five years after my accident.

I hope these ideas will help you discover your great turnaround long before that. If I can, you can too. I'm nobody special, I don't have a university degree, I struggled through school, as a matter of fact, with the help and encouragement of my therapists, I went back to school and graduated grade 12 at the age of 37. It was both very humbling and a great feeling at the same time. I was also awarded the Lieutenant Governor's award for community volunteering.

I hope this book will help you take months or even years off your recovery time. Let my failures be your lessons and let my victories be your inspiration.

This book is in no way intended to replace advice of any medical professional.

Forrest

"Become addicted to constant and never-ending self-improvement."
— *Anthony J. D'Angelo, Author*

"What is important is not what happens to us, but how we respond to what happens to us."
— *Jean Paul Sartre, Writer and Philosopher*

My car ... or I mean, what's left of it.

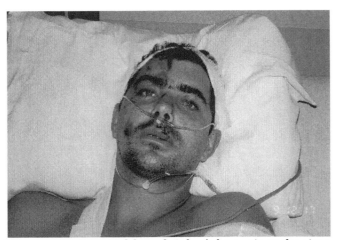

This picture is me, although I don't know it at the time.
Visit Youtube: Forrest Willett, for the full video

"Desire is the key to motivation, but it's the determination and commitment to an unrelenting pursuit of your goal—a commitment to excellence—that will enable you to attain the success you seek."
— Mario Andretti, Race Car Driver

Chapter Four
At the Hospital

This section pertains particularly to the caregiver
This can be a very confusing time for everyone, so it's important to remain calm at the hospital. If your loved one has had a stroke or has been hospitalized for any reason, you must realize that they are going through a very stressful time. Adding your own stress and fears on top of that will only compound the problem. Just know that they are in the best place they can be, with the best care available to them at this time.

In the unexpected event of an accident, word spreads like wildfire. So you may find yourself in the hospital with many other concerned people, friends, co-workers, relatives, neighbors and other family members. Everyone will be experiencing different emotions that come and go at different times.

I can't imagine what family members must go through, so I asked my wife, friends and some family members about their emotions at the time of my accident. They said that time stood still and things they once took for granted were changed forever. Their priorities changed.

Here are some more feelings they experienced...

Shock and denial— You may have a hard time believing what just happened is real. You're in shock or you can't believe that this just really happened. Everything is a blur and you may have a hard time remembering information or conversations.

Fear and panic — These are common reactions after a traumatic event. Your fear is intense because of the unknown. Will he live? Will he die? The panic continues until the patient is stabilized.

Some of the feelings you may experience include a racing heart, inability to sleep, decreased appetite and a lot of crying. Shock, numbness, disbelief, panic, helplessness, and hopelessness are a few more common feelings. Your emotions may feel like you're on a roller coaster.

Anger — Many people feel angry and wonder "Why did this happen?" They may be angry at themselves for different reasons, they may be angry at the doctor for not getting the answers that they want to hear. Try to have some compassion. The doctors and nurses are trying their best to help your loved one survive and are under a lot of stress themselves. So it's important to control your anger and aggression in the hospital. You may even be asked to leave at some point if you cannot control your emotions.

Guilt — This is another reaction that many people feel. Some people feel they may have been able to prevent the accident, even though in most cases they could not. Some people ask, "Why could it not have been me instead of them?" Especially if there is a child involved.

You may also experience visitors whom you've not seen in years but, for some reason, also feel guilty, whether it's for not keeping in touch or something that happened in the past that was not cleared up. Whatever their reason is, it may be their guilt that has brought them to the hospital.

I have seen for myself a father coming to the bedside of his son in the hospital. His mother told me the father had not been around for 15 years and I would imagine it was guilt that brought him there.

Anxiety — Your anxiety may be floating along like a feather in the wind, up one minute with the hope of recovery and down the next with complications and setbacks. This is where it's very important to express your feelings and concerns with your family, friends, and doctors. These feelings may go on for weeks and change day-to-day, hour-to-hour. It may seem as if you are in a dream from which you hope you will soon wake up.

Fatigue and sleeplessness are experienced by many people in these conditions and they only compound the situation; try to stay well rested.

> *"One today is worth two tomorrows; never leave that till tomorrow which you can do today."*
> *— Benjamin Franklin*

Reduce stress at the hospital

What can be done at the hospital to reduce the fears and anxieties of yourself and those around you, and also make your stay a little less stressful?

For the caregiver

Remain calm. Panic and anxiety will only make the situation worse. When friends or family members see you panicking, they will also panic. Then the anxiety is in control, not you.

If you have a crowd of visitors, ask them to go home and let them know that you will notify them with any news.

Put someone who is not at the hospital in charge of all notifications. They will be able to phone people and be a contact person that concerned people can phone for information. This is a lot better than having people calling the hospital steadily or looming around the waiting room.

This person could also be in charge of coordinating people that want to visit. It's important not to overwhelm the patient because they need to rest in order to heal properly. Too many visitors in one day can cause fatigue and stress, which will slow the healing process.

Give the main caregiver a break. You cannot expect a husband, wife, mother or father to sit at the bedside of an injured person for days and weeks on end without it affecting their own health, be it mental or physical. They must take a break or they could end up in the hospital.

Try to have some relief caregivers that can sit with the patient while the main caregiver(s) take a break, even if it's just going for a walk and getting some fresh air. I would suggest going out for dinner with a friend or relative or getting a good night's sleep in your own bed to help get your mind off things for awhile. A well deserved mental break will help you see things more clearly.

When people come to visit, always meet them in the hallway first for a quick briefing. Make them aware of what they are about to see. This will reduce some anxiety or shock, especially if the person is disfigured like I was.

My teeth were missing and my face looked like a swollen basketball covered in blood and bruises with many tubes and wires all over my body. Although I have no memory of being in the hospital whatsoever, I have heard stories of other people who do remember, and of people coming to visit others in similar situations as mine.

One that sticks out was a grandmother coming to see her grandson without first being briefed. She broke out hysterically crying, "Oh my poor baby look at your face, I can't believe it, it doesn't even look like you!"

That kind of visit compounds the stress and fears of not only the patient but the grandmother and whoever else was in the room. If she had been briefed as to what she might see, she may have been able to stay calm and keep her composure and that would also keep the patient calm.

The other thing to keep in mind is that if you're going to talk about the patient in a negative way, go out in the hall and shut the door. Just because a person is unconscious doesn't mean they don't know you're there and can't hear what you're saying. So keep your conversations positive. Never talk negatively about the person in front of them, or at all.

What I mean by this is don't announce to the visitor, "Things don't look too good for Billy" or "The doctor thinks he may not be able to speak again".

These are just negative thoughts. Get them out of your head and think positively, because good things will come. I have met many people who were told they would not talk or walk again and they are now talking and walking just fine.

When speaking to the patient, assume that he or she understands what you are saying. Speak in a comforting, positive, and familiar way. Speak clearly and slowly about familiar people and memories. And when I say speak slowly, I don't mean in slow motion. I just mean slow enough for the person to understand, the patient is not deaf or stupid! Remember, the person has not lost their intelligence, it may just take them a little longer to comprehend what is being said.

If a person is in a coma, perhaps you could play their favorite television show or music. A friend of mine, Sam, was in a coma for months and said, "Do not ever underestimate the power of positive talk when you are in a coma." He went on to tell me that his wife was beside him every day, always talking positively to him, reading to him, playing music and watching the television just as if he was there watching it with her. And it was worth all of the time she spent with him. They now have a great life together and a beautiful daughter.

Get a notebook or day-timer and write down important

information. You can use this to keep track of questions you want to ask the doctors and other healthcare professionals. So often they are in and out very quickly while dealing with the patient and it slips your mind to ask the question you have been waiting to ask until after they have left the room.

It is also helpful to share this information with the patient in the future and allow them to gauge how far they have come along in their journey. This can be very positive for their self-esteem and outlook on life in a world that does not seem very positive from a patient's view looking outward at this time.

Look at examples in your own life. If you were to go to the gym for a work out, and then returned home and looked in the mirror, you wouldn't see any changes. The second and third day would be the same result, with no changes. Now if you kept up this routine for three months and looked in the mirror, you would see a drastic change, not only physically, but your self-esteem would skyrocket.

Express your feelings. Talk to your family and friends about how you are feeling. This will help relieve a lot of stress when you are feeling overwhelmed, and remember, it's okay to cry.

When visitors are present, focus on the patient. Keep the number of visitors to one or two people at a time. Visits should be kept short. Turn off the television and radio while visiting. Too many distractions can overwhelm the patient.

"Never think that you're not good enough yourself. A man should never think that. People will take you very much at your own reckoning."
— Anthony Trollope, British Novelist

Chapter Five
Coming Home

Being discharged from the hospital or rehabilitation center may be a big relief for some people, but it may also be a little frightening for the patient. It may sound odd, but some patients feel more comfortable in the hospital than they do coming home. In the hospital, the patient may feel safe and secure and confident that no one is going to harm them. The hospital may be a security blanket and for some it is the only familiar place they know at the time.

For me, coming home was a difficult experience because it no longer felt comfortable and familiar. It was a new world for me. Little things that once seemed normal, such as our dog barking, now sent me over the moon. When he would bark, I would almost jump out of my skin with fear and anxiety. The same would happen when someone slammed the door. I had so much anxiety built up that it took very little for me to feel overwhelmed.

There were new faces in my house that I did not recognize, such as home care workers and personal support workers. This was all very new to me in an uncomfortable way, having a stranger bathe me while my wife was at work. Even the bathtub was different, now outfitted with a chair and handlebars on the wall. I have to say it took some getting used to, this new home of mine.

I don't know why but little distractions such as a dishwasher running, or the noise from the television or radio would distract me to the point where I could not understand what someone was saying when they were talking to me. Often I would just nod my head with a blank stare on my face as if I understood what they were saying, thinking "Your lips are moving, but I have no idea what you're saying".

So keep this in mind when you come home with your loved one. It is important to have a minimal amount of distractions. We already have a problem with being distracted easily. This can also be compounded with memory problems. Yes, I'm admitting it. "Sorry" to all the doctors and therapists who explained this rationale to me many times and I doubted it every time. I can now look back and put it all together and I hope this will save you a lot of time and frustration.

I would be angry with my wife and say things like, "Why the hell didn't you tell me John called?" And she would reply, "I did tell you when you were watching the television this morning." You see, I was distracted but I would just blame everything on a bad memory. It was an easy out and I constantly used the excuse, "I forgot".

So remember, the less distractions you have, the less you will hear yourself say "I forgot".

To the patient

Just as you have a team leader in the hospital, it is also important to have someone in the beginning that can do things such as keep family, friends and co-workers informed of your progress, as well as co-ordinate visits and phone calls. Once you come home from the hospital, it is easy to become overwhelmed by the sudden attention from family, friends and relatives. Try to have short visits and have a break in between visits. Fatigue is one of the major problems that come with a brain injury and this is something that I still struggle with. I could not understand why I slept more than my two-year-old son. Try to understand that just talking with a visitor for 10 minutes can make you feel as tired as running a marathon. It sounds odd but it is true.

I think it is very hard for someone who has not had a brain injury to understand what is going on. You may hear comments such as "Christine looks great now that she is home, but I just can't understand why she wants to sleep all day". This is very often seen as laziness, but I can tell you it is not. After suffering a brain injury you need a lot of rest to heal. But you also must understand that the things you took for granted before, such as your everyday routine, will now be a major effort. In trying to do those things, fatigue just compounds your frustration. Someone once said to me there are twenty-seven steps to make a peanut butter sandwich from opening the bag of bread to eating the sandwich. But when you do it everyday it seems as easy as 1-2-3.

Remember to surround yourself with positive people who are willing to help. Just look at anyone who has had a successful recovery and you will see that they did not do it alone. You will see that they had a great support team made up of friends and family and professionals who were all positive and supportive during the good times and bad. Have you ever driven a car and discovered that the emergency brake was on? Did you push harder on the gas? Probably not, you just released the brakes and went further faster. Everyone I know who has had a successful recovery of any extent had to release the human emergency brakes that were slowing them down. What I mean is that you need to get rid of, or spend considerably less time with people that drag you down and fertilize the weeds of depression and hopelessness.

To the caregiver
When your loved one comes home, allow him/her the time to rest and heal. You may even have to schedule some rest times into their day-timer, as I had to do. If it wasn't scheduled in my day-timer, I usually wouldn't rest, and then I would be too tired to even think. I would usually rest between one and three o'clock; that is when I was the most tired during the day.

When someone offers help, accept their help because you can't do this alone. You have a long road ahead of you so please take my advice, and accept the help being offered, but be specific about how this person can help. Allow them to stay with your loved one while you go shopping or prepare meals. If you have other children, allow a friend to take your children to a movie or play outside while you can get some well needed rest.

People must realize that it is not just the brain-injured person's life that has been turned upside-down, the whole family is affected. The whole family will have to adjust to this new life. Yes it does suck! The sooner you accept what has happened, the sooner you can begin your journey to recovery.

Chapter Six

Some People with a Brain Injury Will Not See a Hospital

I have met many people with a brain injury who were not officially diagnosed at the time of their injury. After some people have hit their head, they think it is just a headache and will go away. They don't take it seriously until someone points out irregularities in the person's behavior or cognitive abilities.

Here are a few examples why people did not seek immediate medical attention and their reasons for it. One woman was doing laundry with a stackable washer and dryer. She opened the dryer door, bent down, and pulled the laundry from the washing machine. As she stood up quickly, she knocked herself out on the dryer door. Luckily she had a friend with her to explain what happened when she came to. She took a few aspirins and laid down until the headache went away. She was a school teacher who in the coming months found she could no longer do her job. She is doing well now even though she is not teaching anymore.

Another person I met slipped on some ice on the sidewalk leaving him with a large lump on the back of his head. Not thinking much about it, he took aspirin and tylenol for a few days thinking he could shake it off. As it turned out, the only thing he shook off was his relationship with his wife. She noticed the differences in his behavior and thinking and brought it to his attention, which made him angry. He was in denial and refused any help for years, eventually finding himself living alone. He is making tremendous progress now that he has accepted what has happened and is working on improving his behavior and cognitive abilities. I wish him all the best in the future. He is a good person who just needs some help.

If you know of someone who has had an injury to the head, please talk to them about seeking help or at least getting it checked out. The following are some of the common symptoms you may see in a person who has had a brain injury. Remember everyone is different - these are only some common symptoms. The best person to consult and confirm this would be a doctor.

Symptoms:
- Changes in, or unequal size of pupils
- Chronic or severe headaches
- Coma
- Fluid draining from the nose, mouth or ears (may be clear or bloody)
- Loss of consciousness, confusion or drowsiness
- Loss or change in sensation, hearing, vision, smell or taste
- Memory loss
- Mood, personality or behavioral changes
- Restlessness, clumsiness or lack of co-ordination
- Speech and language problems, eighty to one hundred percent of people will have some sort of communication problem

These are just some of the symptoms a person with a brain injury may be experiencing. Again I am not a doctor so if you notice these symptoms in a person please get them to a doctor.

> *"The secret of success is doing the common*
> *things uncommonly well."*
> *— John Davidson Rockefeller Sr., American Oil Magnate*

Chapter Seven
When Will I be Normal Again? What is Normal?

These are some questions I found myself asking again and again. It took a long time to realize there is no right or wrong answer to these questions. My brain injury and depression made me question what society teaches us from an early age about is the idea of normal. Here in North America most of us are brainwashed to think that "normal" is having a wife, two and a half kids, a dog and a mortgage. Just like a perfect family on a television show.

So now when I hear someone ask the question, "Will he or she ever be normal again?" I don't have the answer they are looking for. You see everyone's version of normal is different. Can someone with a brain injury and depression learn to have a relatively normal social life? I think that would depend on the extent of their injuries and how that person defines a social life. If someone is very shy and does not have a brain injury, is he or she more or less normal than a very outgoing person with a brain injury? There is no one-size-fits-all way of behaving for anyone in the world.

The person who cuts my hair is openly gay. Is he normal? Absolutely he is. Does this bother me? Not one bit.

20 years ago people may have said that was not normal, and nowadays it has become very normal and acceptable. As times change, so do people's perception of what normal means to them.

I now have fewer rules as to how people live their lives, although it took a near death experience to change the way I thought. I think I am a better person for it. This kind of thinking also reduced a lot of stress on me by not worrying so much about how other people are living their lives.

Before my injury I would often say to people, "Get over it", to whatever problem they may have, whether it was a sore back or a relationship breakup. I would say "It's not normal to be whining about your problems for so long".

I can now say that it has been several years since I have said "Get over it". Back then I didn't know anything about brain injuries, depression, anxiety or any other type of mental illness. I now know you don't just "Get over it". If I met someone who stuttered quite a bit or forgot what they were saying in the middle of a conversation, I would think to myself "That's not normal," and here I am today doing the exact same thing and believe me it is now normal to me. I think if everyone stopped comparing themselves to what they see on TV and had fewer rules for how other people live their lives, the world would be a better place.

"Confidence is; going after Moby Dick in a rowboat, and taking the tarter sauce with you. A Bull Fighter who goes in the ring with mustard on his sword."
— Zig Ziglar, Author and Speaker

Chapter Eight

Where are all my Friends?

"You miss 100% of the shots you don't take."
— Wayne Gretzky

A few years after my accident I was questioning where all my friends were. It seems they had disappeared and left me. I could count the remaining friends on one hand and they are still there for me today. Thank you Johnny, Denis and Bob for sticking it out with me and not giving up, and also for your sense of humor.

What happened? Taking a step back and looking at things with you right now I can honestly say that I drove some of them away with my constant negativity and self-pity. All I wanted people to know was how bad things were for me, and let me tell you that gets old really fast. I spent more time with my negative thoughts than I did with my family and friends.

I also can tell you that in the early years of my recovery, I wasn't genuinely interested in other people and their feelings. I focused totally on myself. I also talked a lot about how my brain injury had ruined my life and I would be better off dead. I would often argue with people, and after doing that for awhile I was totally by myself and alone.

Some friends were afraid or confused, not knowing what to do, say or expect so the easiest thing for them to do was disappear. That is human nature and has nothing to do with you. Don't take it to heart as I did. Let it go, just let it go.

Some friends just move on in life whether you have a brain injury or not. They meet different people and find different interests. Don't take this personally.

If you are a friend of the injured person, my plea is for

you to stick it out through the good times and the bad. Remember you are friends and there is something about this person that brought you together in the first place. Just try to remember those good qualities that are still inside.

Looking back, I can give you some tips on things to avoid and things that helped me with my friendships.

Things that drove friends away (Avoid these at all costs)

- I interrupted people to get what I wanted to say out there
- I asked people very personal and inappropriate questions
- I wouldn't listen to or take advice and suggestions from other people.
- I wouldn't accept my friends' offers to help
- I did not think before I spoke, and said a lot of things that I should have kept to myself
- I have to admit my frontal lobe editor took a leave of absence.

Things that helped mend and create new friendships

- I worked on accepting myself just the way I was
- I became a good listener; people would then listen to what I also had to say
- I joined a support group that was a tremendous help
- I learned to think before speaking; this way I did not say things I would regret
- I learned to avoid sharing all of my negative thoughts with other people

Chapter Nine
Letter to My Friends

If I could write a letter to my friends back then, this is what it would say...

Dear friends and family,

I am here with you, I really am. Although it may not look like me or sound like me, it is still the same old me inside.

This body is just a vessel to get around in. The engine inside (my heart and soul) is still the same. I am in here and I can understand what you're saying, I just cannot reply at this time in the way you are used to. Please do not abandon me, for your love and acceptance is all I crave.

I am scared to death and don't know what to do, so please bear with me in the months and years to come. I need you now more than I have ever needed you in my life. Your presence alone has more healing power than any medical device and your love and support will guide me through these rough times. Don't give up on me as I have not given up on you. Although I may not smile I want you to know your presence makes my day, and your smile is as soothing as the warm sun on my face. When you smile at me, please be genuine. It breaks my heart to see that awkward forced smile that tells me you are scared and unsure (I can tell by the look in your eyes). Remember you are still the same friend that I always knew. Just smile.

Talk to me as you have always talked to me but just be clear. Don't get upset if you have to repeat yourself as it takes a little longer for me to process things. I'm not deaf, you do not have to yell. I still have my intuition, that "gut feeling" that for some reason I did not lose. So I can tell if you're talking to me like a baby. What you are doing is stepping on my fingers when I'm trying to get up, and you are keeping me down. "The greatest exercise for the human heart is to reach down and lift up another".

I may say things from time to time out of fear or anger that may hurt your feelings and make you question our friendship. This too will pass with time. Please remind me when I'm out of line, don't just leave me and walk away never to return. Make me aware of the hurt I have caused you in a gentle way.

I'm not crying because I feel so sorry for you, I'm crying for me. "Poor me, why me, this can't be happening to me". I want you to know this is a phase I'm going through, "Me-me-me " but it will pass as well. It is just a phase, a phase that I will need your help with. I cannot do this alone.

You'll get frustrated because I'm not the same person I was last week or last month. I have changed, give me time and I will change again for the better. Love me and encourage me, remind me of things we used to do, show me pictures. My hope is that if I was on the receiving end of this letter I would show you kindness and compassion.

Thank you, my friends!

Chapter Ten
Letter to Myself

If I could write a letter to myself and send it back in time, this is what it would say:

Dear Forrest,

Get up out of that bed of misery and pity that you lay in all day. You have a wonderful life and so much runway ahead of you; a beautiful wife and son that love you more than you can imagine and all you're doing is pushing them away.

Stop and look around at what you're doing to yourself, it doesn't have to be this way. There are better days ahead, you just have to open your mind to see them.

When one door closes another one opens. You are so focused on the door that closed you cannot see the open one.

I would suggest you get rid of all the negative influences in your life. You know the ones. The ones you think are your friends who bathe in the same puddle of pity as you, almost as if it's a contest to see who has it worse "You think you've got it bad? Well let me tell you what happened to me last night".

Please say goodbye to all of your excuses. Write them down and burn the paper or tear it up and flush it down the toilet never to be seen again.

I can tell you from the future that I have met hundreds of people struggling emotionally and I see one thing in common with people who do not succeed in their recovery and that is their massive list of excuses or poor me stories.

These are the exact same things that are stopping these people as well as yourself from a speedy recovery to emotional success.

I know it is difficult to drop or dismiss these alibis or excuses because they are part of you. After all, you are the one who thought them up, they are your little babies and you are the one who formed a habit of continually using them.

When this happens you become attached to these alibis and use them as a crutch or as an excuse for why you can't do something.

And Forrest, here is a list of some of your famous excuses. See if any sound familiar:

> *I forgot....*
> *I can't read it because I have a brain injury.*
> *I can't talk on the phone because I stutter....*
> *I can't meet new friends because of my anxiety and depression...*
> *If only I had parents who loved me....*
> *If only I had a good education.....*
> *If only I were younger....*
> *If only I had been given a chance....*
> *If only I had someone to help'me...*
> *If only everybody wasn't against me...*
> *If only I could just get a lucky break...*
> *If only people understood me....*
> *If only that accident didn't happen...*
> *If only there was a magic pill to fix my brain...*
> *If only other people would listen to me...*
> *If only I had the courage to look in the mirror and admit to myself that I am the one, and the only one, bringing these problems on myself.*

It is time to give up all of the blaming and excuses, and by giving up all of the blaming and excuses and I mean all, it will be the beginning of a new life and believe me when you can do that, a load will be lifted off your mind. You'll feel better physically and emotionally. I'm only speaking to you from experience, so please give it a try and let them go. Only then can you truly begin to heal.

For most of my life I blamed my mother for abandoning me at the age of six and leaving me with an abusive father. The only person this blaming was hurting and dragging down was me. It was my seven hundred pound boulder I had to push to school everyday and then turn around and push home. Once you give up all of your blaming and excuses, there are no more boulders to push and life is no longer a struggle.

Go see a psychologist or therapist as soon as you can. This will help you in your progress. Don't be shy or embarrassed about it, because life turns out to be amazing.

Pay more attention to your therapists from the beginning and take an active role participating in whatever strategies they are trying to teach you. You will find out they are not around forever so accept their help now.

Don't get stressed out and make yourself sick over an upcoming neuro-psych test. It turns out they were the only tests in your life that you didn't have to study for! All you have to do is be yourself.

If you're faced with an upsetting or confusing decision, ask the other party if you can think about it for a day. This will stop you from making wrong and impulsive decisions and save you a lot of grief and money. Remember, the quickest way to find something that is lost around the house is to go buy a replacement.

Spend more time with your son. I know you're tired and you want to sleep, so sleep on the couch with him while he is watching TV. Just spend more time with him and let him know you love him every day.

Kiss your wife every day and let her know how much she means to you. Think about the last 10 things you say before you leave the house.

Give hugs to everyone you love, and show them love as if it may be the last time you see them. You know from experience that it may be.

And finally find something funny to laugh at every day and keep smiling.

Chapter Eleven
Hoarders

"The people who get on in this world are the people who get up and look for the circumstances they want, and if they can't find them they make them."
— *George Bernard Shaw, Playwright, winner of the Nobel Prize in Literature*

If you have not seen the hit television show *Hoarders*, it is based on people's problems in hoarding useless junk. When you listen to the people's stories they all start the same way ... collecting an item here, and soon they are overwhelmed. It seems like there is no help for them because their lives are taken over by their all-consuming clutter. Eventually they need an intervention from friends and family and also some professional help.

I didn't notice this in myself until I had seen the show a few times. Wow, me a hoarder? I can now say I was a hoarder, but not for collecting junk around my house. No, it was much worse. I was a mental hoarder, collecting and hanging onto all sorts of junk in my mind, negative thoughts and emotions. (Oh no, I'm going to be late for my doctor's appointment. I wish this damn traffic would hurry up. I forgot to call Gary back. Nothing works out for me. Something bad has to happen soon, things have been going too good for too long.) We've all had days like this, but when every minute of every day is filled with thoughts like these, your mind becomes completely full. It is very hard to sort through the clutter and very frustrating when you think about it, so it is much easier just to give up, isn't it?

I did not know at the time how harmful this was to myself, my family and most of all my recovery. With the help of Dr. Davidson I found that having a clear mind was a major step towards recovery, not only for my mental health but also with my relationships. He showed me that I could slow down, clear my mind of all thoughts except a few important ones and see the world a lot more clearly.

This is where I learned to use the three D's:
Do it, Delegate it or Dump it.

Dr. Davidson shared a lot of wisdom with me that made sense. I soon learned that not everybody can do everything but everybody can do something.

So if you're thinking of something that has to be done, don't just keep it in your memory bank or on the back burner. You can either do it right away and get it out of the way, or delegate it to someone who can do it. Don't be afraid to ask for help. You will be surprised at how many people are willing to help you.

The final thing you can do is dump it. Get it right out of your mind if it is not important. Just throw it in the trash bin and forget it. That's the one I had the biggest problem with. All of these little things of very little importance were taking up space and cluttering my thoughts, keeping me on an emotional roller coaster.

My hope is that if you are an emotional or mental hoarder, you will seek some help and learn to clear the clutter that is holding you back on your road to recovery.

If you have not seen the show 'Hoarders', take the time to watch it once and see the similarities between yourself and the people on the show. See the positive changes people have made in their lives once the clutter is gone and how great they feel. It is like they have been given a second chance in life. You too can experience this just by getting rid of the mind clutter - it is very simple.

I did not say easy, I said simple.

Chapter Twelve
A Case for Organization

Are you aware that physical and emotional clutter can leave a "cloud" hanging over your head, and your life? A person with an acquired brain injury will usually have a larger "cloud" than people without an injury. Life can be overwhelming in the best of circumstances but tackling daily chores and dealing with schedules are definitely more challenging when you have an acquired brain injury.

Studies have shown that a patient's adjustment can be deeply impacted by mild impairments such as short-term memory. The extra effort, vigilance, and concentration needed to compensate for mild deficits can result in an enormous fatiguing effect. This causes a continuous drain on energy levels and results in chronic fatigue. Intellectual functions such as short-term memory tend to deteriorate as fatigue increases, which can lead to a vicious cycle of inadequacy, discouragement, irritability and depression.

Some common side effects of brain injuries are difficulties with memory, mood and concentration. Other side effects include significant deficits in organizational and reasoning skills, learning, cognitive, and executive functions. Some adjustments and accommodations during the recovery period will be important, and they may last a lifetime in some cases. The need for assessing, implementing and maintaining an organizational plan is a crucial step for those living with an acquired brain injury.

Most individuals with an acquired brain injury, who are living in their own home, will have the assistance of several support staff and workers as well as family members and friends who visit. Unfortunately, not everyone will have the same idea as to where to find and put things. It is primarily up to you to decide where items should be kept. Your unique needs should always be the priority of anyone who enters the home.

You might be performing housekeeping chores, such as preparing meals or cleaning, either alone or with assistance. This will go a lot more smoothly if everyone is aware of your individual needs and knows where to find stuff and put things back. I know how stressful it was when everyone wasn't on the same page.

Sometimes a professional organizer may need to be hired. They can assess your unique needs and address any concerns of anyone involved with you at home. The process can be as simple as reorganizing the kitchen cupboards and placing labels or instructions throughout the home. Or it can be more complex and involve de-cluttering and organizing the entire home. A professional organizer can also create, implement and display daily structured plan sheets, set up your Personal Device or Smartphone with scheduled reminders and appointments, move furniture to assist in your mobility needs and post color-coded information or reminders throughout your home.

To have the best recovery outcome, a collaborative approach among everyone helping to support the patient is desirable. Protocols such as information sharing (a general communication binder) as well as identifying areas of responsibility for all involved should be assessed and implemented.

It is essential to encourage the patient to have an increased level of independence from the start by implementing an organizational plan for them, as well as anyone else who is involved in their care. The type and level of support is as unique as the person and their experience.

The goals of an organizer normally include:
- Maximizing the patient's mobility (assessing

furniture placement) and activities of daily living including communication

- Implementing plans to improve their attention span, memory, judgment and physical function
- Educating the patient, their family and support staff of their individualized needs
- Reducing stimulation in the environment such as activity and noise levels
- Providing routines for patients

Chapter Thirteen
What Color are Your Eyes?

Jack Canfield shared with me an exercise that turned out to be a big game changer in my life and it can help clean up your messes and in-completes too.

I was instructed to go through my house with a sheet of paper and write down every little thing that irritated me, such as the leaky tap, returning a drill that I borrowed, and getting rid of an old broken television in the garage.

Now that you have your list, go through the house and fix every single thing, one at a time. I did this myself and it took me about a week. Afterwards, I couldn't believe how much better I felt about myself once I didn't have these little things irritating me anymore.

The reason for this exercise is that if we consistently settle for the little things we don't want or like in life, we live in resignation and resign ourselves to not having what we want in life. Once all these little things are cleaned up, you begin to build some momentum and can start tackling bigger things that have been irritating you.

A few of my biggest irritations were questions I had carried my whole life, allowing them to consume my energy. "What color are your eyes?" was probably the most difficult question I have ever asked. The reason is because my mother and I have had virtually no contact with each other for 35 years. I wanted to know the color of her eyes and if she loved me and thought of me often.

Growing up, I was always told by my father that she wanted nothing to do with me. Yet something inside me did not want to believe that, so I carried the irritation around with me for 35 years until I confronted the issue and picked up that 10,000 pound telephone and called her. As it turns out, she did think of me often and missed me tremendously. We are now in the process of building a relationship and getting to know each other, there is a lot of catching up to do.

I would challenge you to make a list of things around the house that are irritating you, tackle them and then move on to take care of the bigger things in life that have been irritating you.

I can share with you there is no better feeling than having questions answered that you've worried about for years. When in doubt, check it out. Don't torture yourself mentally for years as I did.

Ask yourself this question, if you only had one phone call left to make in your life right now who would you call? What would you say? And what are you waiting for?

Just so I don't leave you hanging, her eyes are hazel...

These are just some of the common feelings I was experiencing as I began my journey of recovery:

Grieving
If you can understand the stages of grieving that a person going through a traumatic event may experience, it can make everyone's life a little easier and remove some of the questions you may be having about what is going on.

Denial (not the river in Africa)
When I look back now and talk about it with my wife, I was probably in denial for well over a year, but probably closer to two. Denial is a term used to describe the tendency to minimize undesirable personal characteristics, behaviors or events that have happened in your life.

You may try to do everything you did before and say

things like "There's nothing wrong with me, I'm fine." Those are words I have said many times. In the dictionary, denial is described as a refusal to grant the truth of the statement or allegation. This is an unconscious defence mechanism characterized by a refusal to acknowledge painful realities, thoughts or feelings.

In my world it meant sweeping my problems under the rug or just hoping, if I held out long enough, that all of my troubles would go away.

"Don't worry, just give me a few weeks and I'll be back to normal" or "I'm just going through a phase" and "Not me, I'm not brain injured or depressed, that is just a term the doctors use," were comments that I have made many times. All in the hope that I was just going through a phase and things would get better in a few weeks. But if you're not careful, those weeks can turn into months and then years.

I had no idea that denial was preventing me from recognizing and dealing with the problems I was having and only postponing my journey of recovery.

The quicker you can get out of the denial stage, the sooner you can begin to recover. Look in the mirror and say to yourself, "I have a brain injury and depression and I will work as hard as I can to recover as soon as I can, with the tools that are available to me at this time."

If you can't admit it to yourself, how can you admit it to other people who are trying to help you? If you say "I'm fine, it's ok," why would people help you?

If you are sinking fast and in denial, you are simply "Rearranging the deck chairs on the Titanic." You can only pretend to be ok for a short period of time before you drown.

The secret to getting help is found in three small words, "I need help."

Anger

I was angry with everyone that I came into contact, whether they knew it or not. And this was for many different reasons that didn't make a lot of sense when I look back now. I think the number one reason I was angry with people, was that they didn't understand what I was going through. I was angry with myself for not being able to understand what was going on inside of me too.

Bargaining

I remember thinking "I would give everything I own just to have the old "me" back."

You may also find yourself bargaining when it is too late. For example, if your relationship with someone has gone sour, you may find yourself saying things like, "I will get some help and stop my angry outbursts if you just stay."

Most of the time, when you get to that point, it is too late. So remember this: be kind to your partners, friends, and family members. They too can only handle so much before they reach their breaking point.

Isn't it funny how when we are just about to lose something we give it more value for example many people who hate their job all of the sudden find goodness and benefits in that job the day they are told they are going to be fired and quickly change their attitude, my advice would be fine the goodness in your life today.

Guilt

Guilt was explained to me by one of my doctors as the feeling you get when you violate your own standards. You may feel that you've done something wrong and inside you know you want to fix it. You may also feel regretful for something you have done or something that has happened in your past.

You may feel guilty for many reasons. Maybe you survived a car accident and the other person did not. I have met people going through this exact problem.

One person I know gets very angry when anyone talks about his accident. He is now brain-injured and in a wheelchair, while his best friend was killed. He carries the guilt around like a 100 pound sack of rocks. You can tell that the guilt is dragging him down, but he does not want to talk about it. I believe he is still in the denial stage.

You may feel guilty about being at home, while your husband or wife is working just to keep the bills paid. I felt guilty for many reasons. I couldn't even read my son a bedtime story. "What kind of father am I?" I would ask myself.

But should I have felt guilty, knowing that I couldn't even read the directions on a can of soup? No, I should not have felt guilty.

I have discovered only good people feel guilty. Bad people, like lifetime criminals, do not feel guilty. So be aware if you are feeling guilty because there is a good person inside.

Depression
This is one of the stages that I believe destroys more people than you can imagine. Once you realize that you are not the same person you once were, you may give up all hope on your future. "It's no use, so why even try?" You may have feelings such as hopelessness, being overloaded, overwhelmed, sad or blue.

You may start to neglect yourself, such as not brushing your teeth or hair, wearing the same clothes for days on end or even not eating.

Or you may go the opposite way and begin overeating, because eating is the easiest way to change the way you feel. Some people use drugs or alcohol, but most people eat too much. Just look around at the people you know. Do you know someone who does not feel good about themself? Someone who is overweight from constantly snacking or overindulging in comfort foods? That food may be the only thing that makes them feel good.

If you or someone you know is suffering from depression, please reach out and help them or let them help you.

Fear

Fear is a feeling of agitation and anxiety caused by the presence or imminence of danger and concern that you are in danger or think you are in danger.

Fantasized Events that Appear Real

That is how my doctor described my fear of being a passenger in a car. I was terrified and would scream and grab the dashboard as if I was about to be in an accident all over again. All I could think of while riding in the car was that it was going to happen again, it was just a matter of time. I was literally making myself sick from the fear and anxiety I had of riding in a car or thinking something bad was going to happen soon.

After a lot of counselling I realized that my fear was just that: a fantasized-event-appearing-real. In my head, I knew it was going to happen again. It has been nine years now and my terrified fear very rarely happens anymore.

I want to share with you that 99 percent of the things I feared did not happen and for the one percent that did, they were not nearly as bad as I thought they were going to be.

Acceptance

This is the final stage of grieving, and the one you should be working towards as soon as possible.

This is when you begin to realize that people admire you for your strength, courage, and wisdom.

This is when I began to love and accept myself unconditionally for who I am and not who I used to be.

This is when I took the focus off my problems and stopped living with the victim mentality of "Oh poor me" and decided I was going to be a survivor, and the best one I could be.

This is when miracles happen. This is a time to look forward to and be excited about. This is the time for you to look at the choices you have.

This is a time to forgive. For me, being able to forgive the person that was driving the car the day of our accident relieved a lot of pain and anger I had been holding for quite some time. I realized you cannot move forward if you are always looking back. You must let go of the past to embrace the future.

I began to let go of the pain and focused on the gain that could be achieved without the emotional baggage weighing me down.

This is when I stopped worrying about what our society thinks about mental illness. I realized that having an uninjured brain was not the secret to happiness.

I had that secret with me all along. It was all in my head. You have everything within you to create the happiness you deserve.

"The art of acceptance is the art of making someone who has just done you a small favor, wish that he might have done you a greater one."
— Russell Lynes

Chapter Fourteen
The Iceberg Effect

"To be yourself in a world that is constantly trying to make you something else is the greatest accomplishment."
— *Ralph Waldo Emerson, Poet and Essayist*

Don't become an iceberg. I was one myself. For years I showed a fake smile and a nod, as if everything was okay. But what people did not know was that just under the water, beneath that little smile, was a huge iceberg of pain, confusion, anger, depression and anxiety to name a few. I would only show 10 percent of who I really was and pushed down and hid the other 90 percent.

If I met someone I knew and could not remember their name, I would fumble my way through it with a smile, nodding my head as if I knew what they were talking about, while inside I was having an anxiety attack trying to remember their name.

I was too embarrassed to ask them their name. They obviously knew me very well, since they were talking to me about things in my past and asking how my family was.

And then I accepted some help from Dr. Davidson, who helped me accept me for who I was and what I was going through. He shared with me that avoidance was the problem, not the solution. As I was hiding behind these little riddles of guessing names and events, my iceberg was getting bigger and I was on course to sink a ship, my own ship.

The first time I admitted to a person "I'm sorry, I don't remember your name right now, I'm just recovering from a brain injury I acquired in a car accident. I know that I know you, but your name is just not clicking right now," I felt the weight of the world lift from my shoulders. It actually felt good to get that out. I thought to myself, nothing bad has happened, the person didn't look at me as if I was an alien. All of the negative thoughts in my head were simply not true.

As time went on, I was able to explain to people what I was going through, and received an amazing amount of support from everyone around me. And with that support, it gave me encouragement to carry on with my recovery in a positive atmosphere, knowing that everyone was behind me and not against me.

So if you feel like an iceberg, reach out and get some help, don't be afraid to say I am sorry or I need some help.

"The best job goes to the person who can get it done without passing the buck or coming back with excuses."
— Napoleon Hill, Author of "Think and Grow Rich"

Chapter Fifteen
Tell the Truth Faster

Most of us are afraid to tell the truth because it's uncomfortable. You may be embarrassed by the emotions you are struggling with at this point in your life, or you may have a fear of hurting your feelings or someone else's by telling the truth.

Telling the truth will free up a huge amount of energy to work on the issues you may be struggling with. Have you ever been to your doctor and said, "I feel fine?" And then left, only to find yourself in the parking lot asking yourself why you did not tell the truth? I call "fine" the four letter F___ word. Many people who say "I am fine" are not telling the truth.

The truth is we are all in the same classroom.

It doesn't matter who you are or where you are from, how much money you have, or don't have, what school or college you went to, what sex you are or the color of your skin. Brain injuries and depression do not discriminate, whether you're 28 or 62.

Most people with a brain injury will have to re-learn **how** to cope. That's right, I said re-learn. All of your intelligence and emotions are still in your head, but now they are like a jigsaw puzzle that has fallen on the floor. You just have to put the pieces back together. Everything is still there, you just have to work on putting it back together.

Sometimes a piece of your puzzle will get kicked under the couch and it will take a little longer to find what you are looking for. But don't give up, it's there. Like an ostrich with its head in the sand, eventually it will have to come out or live a life in a cold, and dark place. You too, must also learn to come out into the sunshine, remove your fears and anxieties, and be willing to take a chance and live a great life.

Chapter Sixteen

Benefits of Going to a Support Group

"I believe in angels because my angels believe in me"

My angels are all the beautiful people I have met over the years at the support groups I've attended.

Getting me to join a support group was very difficult as I was still in the denial stage. "There's nothing wrong with me, I don't need to go to a support group," were the statements I would often make, but the truth was, I needed it more than I knew. Looking back, I wish I would have joined years earlier.

Just to make things clear, a support group can be made up of professionals or volunteers, who have a keen interest in the well-being of people who are going through a rough patch in their lives. Whether it is depression or cancer, know that you are not the only one going through this. I would not consider a bunch of guys sitting around your neighbor's garage drinking beer and solving the world's problems to be your support group. They do not have the knowledge to solve some of the problems that may occur on your journey to wellness. They might say what they would do if they were in your shoes, but they are not. The only good thing about free advice is its price.

No one will know what you are going through on your journey to recovery except you and other people that are experiencing a similar journey. No one will experience the extreme emotions of success, failure, and setbacks on your road to recovery other than the people at the support groups, because like yourself, they are driven to fulfil their dreams of recovery. They also have your best interests in mind and are always willing to help you with your goals.

And like you, they dream of better days ahead.

The first time I went to a support group meeting was a few years into my recovery. It was run by the March of Dimes and recommended to me by my speech therapist, Christine. I was dropped off by a taxicab at our local Legion. As I grabbed the door handle to enter, I was paralyzed with fear, knowing that I was stepping out of my comfort zone and the safety of my own home. I wanted to throw up, my hands and knees were shaking, and I was sweating bullets. I felt flooded by waves of anxiety washing over me. Somehow I mustered up the courage to go in and face the music. I said to myself, "Let's get this over with so I can tell Christine that I went, then I can leave after five minutes." Bailing out and running from my fears as I usually did. So I felt the fear, pulled the door open and went in.

I felt very uncomfortable, tense and uneasy from the anxiety of the unknown. "What are they going to ask me? What if I can't speak properly? What if I screw up, are they going to laugh at me?" All these negative thoughts went through my head. And when I left the meeting? I felt as if a huge weight was lifted from my shoulders and the elephant that was standing on my chest (anxiety) was gone, and my breathing slowed down.

All those negative thoughts were gone. I felt great about myself. Finally, I had found a place where I felt comfortable with who I was and comfortable being myself. It was also a huge relief to realize that I was not alone.

The person running the group introduced me to everyone and made me feel welcomed and comfortable. I am forever grateful to her for that day, and every day that I continue to go to the support groups and support others who have a lot of the same feelings I did.

A great resource for support groups of any kind is meetup.com

"I don't know of any other characteristic more important to achieving success than persistence. Never has there been a time when this incredible virtue has failed to create greatness in the person whose heart and soul has been gallantly given in pursuit of a dream."
— John Assaraf, Author

Chapter Seventeen
Why Me?

Why, Why, Why?

That is the question I have asked myself many times over and I still don't have the answer for it. I realized that I must let go of the past to enjoy today. The answer to the question "Why me?" may never be answered. You won't get very far driving down the highway of life if you are always looking in the rear view mirror.

I've had people say to me in the past that it was unfortunate what happened and all the terrible things I had to go through over the years. I think it would be unfortunate if things didn't happen the way they did because then I would not have met all these wonderful people and been able to help others in ways I never thought possible and finally find true happiness in life.

I am in a much better place now than I was before the accident. I am truly living a happy and fulfilling life surrounded by wonderful people and making great changes in the world, one person at a time. It is hard to explain the feeling I get in seeing a person I have mentored who thought at one time, "This is it. There's no hope for me." And who now is making leaps and bounds in their emotional success and getting excited about what the future holds. To me that is more exciting and fulfilling than chasing the almighty dollar in a rat race job like I did for so many years. If the accident did not happen to me, I would not have known what it is like to be truly happy and enjoy life every day.

The question of "Why me" has been around for centuries and the best response I have heard is from Jim Rohn, in a talk that he did called "Why not you, why not now?" If you have a chance, I suggest you go on YouTube and watch it.

To sum up the talk Jim says, "Why not be happy? Why not learn more? Why not earn more? Why not you? And why not now?" Right now is the perfect time to ask yourself those questions and decide if it is time for you to change and be happy.

Chapter Eighteen
Where's Your Daddy?

When a child loses their connection with a parent emotionally, there is no pharmaceutical company or doctor's prescription that can bring that bond back; it takes time and love.

About eight months after the accident, Julie wanted to go shopping for a few hours with one of her friends but there was no one to watch our son, Hunter. I could not drive, take care of the household bills or even use the stove safely at this point. Surely the one thing I was capable of doing was to watch my own son for a few hours. How hard could it be? I just have to turn on the television to cartoons and lay on the couch for a few hours, right?

Wrong.

Hunter fell asleep on the couch and I went out to the garage. I don't remember why. Soon after, my brother pulled in the driveway and asked if I would like to go for a drive. I said sure and off we went to town. We returned about an hour later not thinking anything was wrong until we pulled down the driveway and saw some cars in the driveway. One of them was a police car, and that's when I got a rude awakening.

Hunter had woken up after I left and my neighbor, who was in her garden, heard Hunter crying and saw him with his arms raised, pushing on the glass door. She immediately ran over to find out what was going on. The house was empty and thinking something was wrong, she called other neighbors to help look for myself and Julie. Back then we did not carry cell phones around like we do today. Everyone was in a panic until I came back home. That is when things really changed.

Over the next few days I was given many talks and interventions from my family, doctors and therapists. After getting everything straightened out, there were no charges from the police. That may have been easier to accept than what was to come. No, not the wrath of my mother-in-law, it was worse. It was determined that I was not fit to keep my own son by myself. In fact, the powers that be determined I was not fit to keep myself with myself at the time, so what followed was 24 hour attentive care until I could prove I could be safe on my own. They called it attentive care. I called it a babysitter.

This incident damaged my self-esteem and the little remaining self-confidence I had left. It was a very depressing time.

Just one mistake can change your whole life in a short time. I wish I could take that day back and I do regret it. This is a very personal and embarrassing thing for me to admit. I just hope this story can serve as a lesson to people to focus on what you are doing and be realistic about what you are capable of. You can see that the one thing I thought I could handle turned out to be my biggest mistake.

Although this was a big wake up call, it wasn't enough for me to make a huge change in my life. That wouldn't happen until I discovered that baseballs don't bounce...

There are only so many toothless grins and chances to be a Superhero to your children. Enjoy them while you can.

"To bring up a child in the way he should go, travel that way yourself once in a while."
— Josh Billings, Author

Chapter Nineteen
Baseballs Don't Bounce

There's an old Chinese proverb that says "Fall down seven times and get up eight." If your journey is anything like mine, you will fall down many times. The important thing is to keep getting back up. If you don't fall down and get back up in life how will you ever have the confidence to know that you can?

Someone once said to me "You've got to roll with the punches". Well sometimes that gets very hard because you ask yourself, when are the punches going to stop coming? Let me tell you they don't, not for a long time. As you can imagine, things were not very good in the first few years and my future was looking very unclear.

Looking back now I can see that I could have reduced a lot of the stress on my family and myself. I also could have excelled in my recovery if we had only known ahead of time some of the obstacles we were going to face. The big turnaround in my life that changed the way I looked at things and dealt with my problems occurred several years into my recovery at Hunters seventh birthday party. This is the day that taking 100 percent responsibility for my life really clicked for me.

I was at the birthday party, but sitting away from the kids because their laughing and yelling would rattle my nerves to no end.

Someone had bought Hunter a baseball glove and ball. He ripped away the colorful wrapping paper and dropped the ball with excitement, looking at the ground as the ball rolled in the dirt. He once again picked up the ball and dropped it on the ground, watching it roll a few feet with a confused look on his face. One of his friends shouted, "Baseballs don't bounce!" Those three words hit me harder than a punch in the stomach.

I couldn't believe how overcome with emotion I became. I had to go into the house because I broke down crying. It was then I realized how selfish I had become. I was so consumed with my own problems and self-pity that I was neglecting the things that were most important in my life, my family. I realized my son was now seven and I had not yet taught him how to skate, ride a bike or even catch a ball. I was also growing further away from my wife. I can see now, looking back, that I spent more time with my negative thoughts than with my own son, essentially abandoning him as well as my wife. I knew if I didn't take charge of my life, it would end up in pieces. I would even find myself divorced, homeless, or worse.

It was then that I made the decision to give up all excuses and start rebuilding my life, giving a 100 percent effort to my recovery, family, and myself.

There are little signs and signals out there that are trying to get your attention every day, and lucky for me I got this one! This time.

My advice to you would be please don't wait for several years to go by before you realize that "Baseballs don't bounce" or whatever your signal or wake-up call in life may be. Luckily for me, my family was still there after all that time. You may not be so lucky, so try to make a change for the better today.

Don't wait.

Chapter Twenty
You Matter

Chances are if you're reading this book you are old enough to realize that your childhood beliefs about Santa Claus and the monster under your bed have changed. As we age, we no longer believe in something that cannot be proven. But the beliefs about yourself should not change just because you have gone through changes.

As we age, many of us start to gain weight, lose hair or our hair starts to turn grey. A common theme seems to be that the older we get, the better we used to be. I'm going to ask you to change that thought and begin to believe in yourself. The older you get, the better you become as a person, and the person you become in the process is worthy of love with so much to offer the world.

You must still believe that you matter to yourself and to your family. You must look into yourself, not outside of yourself and find that you do matter.

Some of the things you deserve to do are:
- Love and accept yourself just the way you are
- Believe in yourself
- Forgive yourself
- Compliment yourself
- Reward yourself
- Discover yourself
- Acknowledge yourself
- Be yourself

Once you begin to do these things for yourself, you'll begin to see that everything in your life becomes a little easier instead of being a struggle. You cannot take care of anything without taking care of yourself, it all starts with you.

This concept took me a few years to adapt to and when I did, I noticed life became easier for myself and other people around me. So start today by doing something for yourself even if it is looking in the mirror and giving yourself a wink saying, "You sure look great today!"

Chapter Twenty-One
Mirror Exercise

Here is a really good mirror exercise I learned from Jack Canfield.

Before you go to bed at night, stand in front of a mirror and begin by making eye contact with yourself. Now:

1. Say your name
2. Appreciate yourself for;
   Achievements you accomplished that day "Applied for a new job"
   Disciplines kept "Walked for 20 minutes"
   Temptations overcome "You didn't eat the butter tarts"
3. Say "I love you" to yourself.
4. Take it in(receive it), and breathe

This may sound odd in the beginning or feel uncomfortable as anything new does. Let the people that you live with know what you're doing so they don't think you're talking to yourself in the bathroom for some unknown reason.

Here is an example of what it might sound like:

"Sofia, I want to appreciate you for the following things today: First I want to appreciate you for going to bed on time last night and not staying up and watching TV which allowed you to get up early today and exercise.

I also congratulate you on having a healthy lunch with no deep-fried foods. You stuck to your commitment of drinking eight glasses of water a day.

And you stayed in a good mood all day, you didn't allow

other people's problems to drag you down and change your mood."

"And one more thing—I love you."

Chapter Twenty-Two
Fatigue, Stress and Worry

These three things can consume you if you don't get them under control quickly. They feed off each other and multiply so fast that they will lead you down a dark and lonely path where you don't want to be. I know. I've been down that path many times. I couldn't focus because I was always too tired from worrying about things that for the most part didn't exist. I was even worrying about the times when I wasn't worrying. I thought, "Something's up, things are going too good today, something bad has to happen to me soon."

Have you ever had a time when you forgot what you were doing, thinking or talking about? When you sometimes forgot even where you were? The names of familiar things slip your mind. You are talking and forget were saying about halfway through the sentence. Words come out of your mouth that you didn't mean to say or they have nothing to do with what you're talking about. These may all be signs of fatigue and stress.

I have learned that fatigue, stress and worry cause the same in return. It is like the candy floss machine at the circus, the more you spin your problems around, the bigger they get. If you notice some of these things happening, you may want to look for some help before it consumes you. These three symptoms will also produce anxiety and depression.

Fatigue, stress and worry are also a factor in many workplace accidents. Many people admit that they will cut corners when under stress or are worried about a deadline.

"Man's mind once stretched by a new idea, never regains its original dimensions."
— Oliver Wendell Holmes, Jr. American Author

Chapter Twenty-Three
Emotional Wounds and Post-Traumatic Stress Disorder

I would like to thank the men and women, young and old, of our armed forces and the first responders, police, fire and nurses including my brother in-law with over twenty years of service, for risking their lives to save ours. The sad fact is that traumatic brain injury is the number one injury of our troops returning from war followed by post-traumatic stress disorder and depression.

I believe there should be more public awareness and support services available for the men and women who serve us. It is the least we can do as a nation, and it sickens me to think of all these people who risk their lives every day, only to return home and be forgotten.

I cannot relate to what it feels like to be in combat, but I can relate to the effects of several traumatic experiences throughout my life, starting as a child, and its effects including Post-Traumatic Stress Disorder (PTSD). This can be a very disabling disorder that can change your life forever. One big problem with PTSD is that it is an invisible disability that people cannot see. I often share with people that I was living on the outside and dying on the inside. The sad thing is that many people just don't get it. This problem is also common among the police and fire fighters. I believe our government should spend more money rehabilitating our people who put their lives at risk each day so we can walk around feeling safe. I do my best to make the invisible visible by bringing these problems into the light.

This is not a new problem, it has been around for years. My good friend, Tim Nesbitt, whom recently passed away, was in World War II and saw the negative effects of PTSD back then and how it changed people's lives.

I first met Tim when I volunteered at the Villa retirement lodge where he lived. We instantly became close friends and had a lot in common. We both enjoyed a good laugh and were born in the same week of March, just 50 years apart. When I told Tim about writing a part in the book about PTSD, he was kind enough to open up and share a story with me.

Tim was 23 years old when he arrived in Normandy, June of 1944. He was with the 443 squadron and they arrived at an air base in Sainte-Croix-sur-Mer, late at night. Most of the fellows were underground, so he took cover with another guy under the back of a big truck to shelter themselves from the shelling. He thought to himself, 'If one of those shells hits the truck, I'm a goner'.

When morning came he heard bagpipes, so he went for a walk to investigate the noise that was coming from a British field hospital. What Tim saw there stayed with him for the rest of his life. There were three commandos brutally injured with life threatening injuries. It was very troubling to see.

When Tim came back to Canada he was sent to see a doctor. She asked him if he felt he had post traumatic stress and he replied no. Now he would change his answer to yes. She just gave him a physical examination and said that he was ok. What she couldn't see were the emotional wounds brought home by himself and his fellow soldiers.

It wasn't until years later that he realized the magnitude of the problem. Tim was at a concert with a brass band and bagpipes. Once the bagpipes started, he was overcome with emotion and all of the bad memories of being overseas flooded back and he had to leave the show. Later that day he had a heart attack, which the doctors believe was brought on by stress.

Post-Traumatic Stress Disorder (PTSD)

What can bring it on?

- War or Terrorist attacks
- Car or plane crashes
- Traumatic brain injury
- Child abuse
- Sudden death of a loved one
- Kidnapping, Assault or Rape
- Witnessing a traumatic event

I thank Tim for sharing his story to help other people and most of all for being a good friend to my son and I. We sure will miss our Tuesdays with Tim.

My good friend
Tim and I

Common symptoms of PTSD:

- Anger and irritability
- Guilt, shame or self blame
- Substance abuse
- Feelings of mistrust or betrayal
- Feeling alienated and alone
- Physical aches and pains
- Depression and hopelessness
- Suicidal thoughts and feelings

Chapter Twenty-Four
Depression

Why does it feel so dirty coming clean about depression?

A few years ago there was an outbreak called H1N1, also known as the swine flu. I received a call from my doctor's office asking me if I would like to be vaccinated. After thinking about it for awhile, I realized that no one had ever phoned to warn me about emotional sicknesses such as depression, anxiety and stress. Why would that be? Emotional sickness causes ten thousand times more damage and kills more people than the swine flu, yet it is something that people rarely talk about. I hope this section of the book can help eliminate some of your stress and worry.

Even as I'm writing this, it feels very odd letting the world know about my dirty little secret of depression. Just a few short years ago I could not even admit it to myself. I thought that if I admitted this secret to myself or accepted the fact that I was depressed, people would think of me differently. I hoped it would just go away on its own, and I had a fear of the stigma and being labelled.

How can he be depressed? He's always smiling and joking. If people only knew how hard it was to wear that fake smile every day and pretend to be a trooper. "Don't worry about me, I'm getting along just fine. Everything is great." That was on the outside.

On the inside it was a totally different story. "I am worried about me, I don't how much longer I can keep this up." It was like I was treading water in the middle of the lake and several boats were passing me by and asking if I'm okay. I kept saying I was fine, but I could only keep it up for so long before I would either drown or have to reach out for help.

I just had no ambition or goals at the time. I remember people coming to visit and they would ask if I wanted to do something. My reply was always "No." Friends would ask how I was doing, and I would often just shrug my shoulders. It did not take long for most of those friends to disappear, which only made my pity party even bigger. "Oh poor me, now my friends don't even come around" Looking back I don't blame people for not wanting to be in that toxic environment with me. I can also see it was me that drove them away.

The stress and anxiety was overwhelming in trying to keep up with this "Everything-is-super" attitude. It was not only mental, it was also very much physical. I often found myself at the doctor's office with many different symptoms, most of which I later found out were related to my depression, stress and anxiety. Here is a list of the common symptoms I had complained to the doctor about:

- Feeling dizzy and lightheaded
- Sweaty palms and underarms
- Tightness in the chest as if I was having a heart attack
- Feeling unsteady, shaky knees
- Dry mouth
- Sore neck and tense neck muscles
- A racing heart like I had just run a race and yet I was sitting on the couch
- Butterflies in my stomach
- Diarrhea caused by a nervous stomach. I should have bought shares in Pepto-Bismol!
- Frequent urination
- Difficulty concentrating on one thing because my mind was racing
- Difficulty sleeping
- Difficulty paying attention

The point I'm trying to make here is that about 70% of the time I went to the doctor for different ailments and I could have avoided most of them by getting to the root of the problem and overcoming my depression.

These were just some of the symptoms. I could go on and on but as I talk with other people, these symptoms seem to be common with many people going through the same situation. My family doctor made a few suggestions. The first was plain old exercise, which turned out to be one of the greatest weapons in this battle. Walking daily does relieve stress and makes you feel better.

My doctor also suggested I see a psychologist for help because I was about to crash and crash hard.

On the outside I was a big strong guy making an excellent comeback from tragedy and on the inside I was a five-year-old child separated from my family in a busy mall, not knowing where to turn and crying for someone to help me find my way.

Along came Dr. Thomas Davidson into my life. Before I met him, he was the last person in the world I wanted to see and I didn't even know him. The reason I didn't want to see him was that I thought I could hang on to the last piece of my self-dignity. Getting me to go see a psychologist was like giving a cat a bath, it was very difficult. "I don't need to go see some quack and lay on a couch going over all my problems. There is nothing wrong with me, just leave me alone." I was still in denial.

The fact is he helped me with my dignity and self-esteem. We all have pictures in our head of what a psychologist looks like or acts like, based on their portrayal in movies. The old white-haired guy with round glasses, smoking a pipe and driving an old Volvo station wagon. When I first met Dr. Davidson, my guard was up, just in case he was a mind reader who could take my brain out and dissect it. Well, he didn't and I was surprised. He was a cool, laid-back and friendly guy, very likeable.

Now that my concerns were eased and my guard was lowered, we could get to work. I won't bore you with the small talk, but what I learned from him can help you overcome one of the biggest obstacles you will face. He showed me that fatigue, stress and worry cannot exist in the presence of complete relaxation. You cannot continue to worry if you relax. So to prevent fatigue, stress and worry, you must learn to rest often. Rest before you get tired. What do you have to lose?

Sounds odd, but it works. So I started to rest every day, putting it in my day timer as if it was an important meeting, and it was.

An important meeting with myself that helped me greatly with my recovery. You can do it anywhere and at any time.

Here are a few examples of relaxation:

Lie down on the floor or couch for ten to fifteen minutes and close your eyes. You don't have to fall into a deep sleep, just turn your head off like a light switch. Imagine you are on a cloud just floating around. Let yourself relax completely. All of your muscles are at ease. Remember, a tense muscle is a working muscle; you are not working here. Relax, you can do this anywhere. At work, during lunch or at home. I often do it right in the airport before I get on a plane. Do people think I'm different? I don't care because it is none of my business what other people think of me. I'm relaxed and they are not.

Talking to yourself is also a great way to relax. Talk to your muscles and tell them to loosen up because everything is okay. Just relax as you do that and you will feel the tension release. I have a great guided relaxation available for free on my website that you can download. (forrestwillett.com)

You can load it on an MP3 player or your phone and listen to it while you're relaxing, just don't listen to it while you're driving.

It really works. I didn't cure my fatigue. I didn't have to cure it. I prevented it.

"Don't just do something, stand there". That's right, just stand there at times or sit down and have some time to yourself. Whether it is two minutes or two hours, just do nothing. My problem was trying to be everything for everybody just to prove there was nothing wrong with me. The problem was I burned myself out trying to make everyone around me happy and prove that I could still do things when I should have been resting. I call this the "Disease to please." I now realize that your body heals when it is resting. You must do things in life and take on new tasks and try different things, but you also need time to relax. Relaxation really helped me with my depression, sleep disorder, pain, anxiety, and it also helped to sharpen my concentration.

By resting frequently, I was able to work on my recovery, fresh and fit. You owe it to yourself to just give it a try. If you don't take the time to relax, you could have trouble at home or at work and get wiped out emotionally and physically. So just relax and watch your worries disappear. It costs nothing to try.

Fatigue or lack of sleep would turn out to be one of my biggest problems from day one. It starts in the hospital. Every hour on the hour they are waking you up and checking your vital signs. People are constantly in your room so it is very hard to get any rest unless they drug you, which they obviously did to me. I was given a morphine pump and was allowed to give myself doses through an intravenous line. My wife said that I would press it constantly, hoping to feel better as I dosed in and out of consciousness. I have no memory of this, but I can picture it happening just to get some rest. Poor sleep continued to be a problem when I returned home because there were now many more distractions to deal with.

Practice 'prepared calm'. My neighbor is a commercial airline pilot and I have talked to him about dealing with stress. How do you keep it together if something bad goes wrong in the air? His reply was they practice prepared calm. Every few months they are tested in a simulator and given every possible negative situation that can occur such as engine failure, loss of cabin pressure or a violent passenger. Once they are subjected to these situations, they are better prepared to deal with them in a calm and cool manner because they know how to handle them.

What a great idea! After our talk I started to review a lot of the negative thoughts I was having and to think how I would handle each situation if they occurred. This really set my mind at ease because I was prepared for anything that was thrown my way. I suggest you try it too. Oddly enough, none of the negative events I prepared for in my mind have ever occurred.

These are my weapons in the Battle on Depression.
What are yours?

Duke University has conducted two studies comparing

Zoloft a popular antidepressant to walking and head-to-head walking briskly three times a week for 30 minutes won over the Zoloft each time also moderate exercise has fewer side effects than antidepressants and it can prevent and treat depression.

If you have not exercised in a while it would be wise to advise and healthcare professional before starting a suitable exercise program to avoid any injury.

Chapter Twenty-Five
Tattoos and Suicide

Tattoos and suicide are two things I would highly recommend you avoid at all costs.

Suicide is the subject that people don't want to talk about so I thought I would break the ice with tattoos. You see the two of them have a lot in common. I know people who have gotten tattoos and people who have attempted suicide and everyone regrets their decision. When I talk to people, they all seemed to have been done on an impulse, either about someone or something. These two decisions were carried out or attempted without putting much thought to the final outcome and later impact. I believe both of them are done as a cry for help or attention in some way.

Suicide is a subject that must be talked about. There have been many people right here in my own little town that have taken their lives, and most of them were men. I believe that if they had someone to talk with about their problems, the outcome could have been different. Suicide is a permanent solution to a temporary problem.

I have been fortunate enough to meet a great person who has attempted suicide. Fortunately he is still with us and he shares his story in the hope that other people will avoid the same situation. This person attempted suicide after an acquired brain injury he received when he fell down a flight of stairs. After the accident, he also suffered from severe depression, another subject that should be talked about without shame.

This man is very intelligent, far more educated than me. I mean this is the kind of guy who could teach chemistry to a chemistry teacher. After his brain injury he became very depressed because he could no longer do his job and what he loved. He lost his job at the lab.

From there he felt that life as he knew it was over. How could this man, a modern-day Albert Einstein, come to such a conclusion? I wanted to know so I asked him what happened. What was the straw that broke the camel's back? He said he became so depressed and frustrated that he could no longer do his job. He felt worthless and he also felt he was a burden to his family, so he decided everyone would be better off without him. One day, as he tells me of his first suicide attempt, he phoned the local hospital and said he had taken a large quantity of pills. He was taken to the hospital and his stomach was pumped out.

The next Saturday he phoned the local hospital and said he had suicidal thoughts. They told him to call back on Monday when he could talk to a counsellor (I'm not making this up). Take into account that this happened over 20 years ago, before they had suicide hotlines and 24-hour counsellors.

He stabbed himself in the heart and slashed his wrists (I have seen the scars and they are scary). He was flown to a hospital by air ambulance and pronounced dead in the air and he was once again revived.

He went on to tell me that "hell" was waiting for him just around the corner, and by that he did not mean death. It was worse, he explained. Worse than the pain and depression that he suffered in the past? What could be worse?

He spent the next 60 days in a mental institution where he was subjected to electric shock therapy and enough drugs to make a zombie out of an elephant. If you thought it was hard to look for a job before, just put that on your resume. No, wait a minute, he didn't have to because when you live in a small town everyone knows what happened and it usually gets blown way out of proportion.

After all of this he still suffers from depression but it is now under control with proper medication. He is also putting what he knows best on paper, writing a massive book about the medicinal uses of exotic plants. I see him a few times a year and I am proud to call him a friend. He is also an inspiration to the many people he shares his story with.

If you know anyone who is sending out a cry for help, please reach out and help them. Just talking with someone over a cup of coffee can mean the difference between life and death. People want to be heard and to share their stories.

For myself, if I said I never thought about suicide, I would be lying. I did think about it on several occasions and I am grateful that I didn't try anything and never went past the thoughts.

I want to share with you what brought me to those thoughts. I think the biggest thing was my inability to see a better future. I thought if this is the way my life is going to be, then I don't want be here anymore. I also felt that I was a burden on my family and I thought they would be better off without me. I just couldn't see any way out of the hole that I had dug myself into emotionally, other than the easy way out. I also want to share with you what stopped me dead in my tracks.

I reached out for help to someone with a similar situation and thoughts, and what they said has stuck with me ever since then. He said if you're thinking about writing a letter about how bad life is and you can't go on any longer, start with a different letter. Write an apology letter to your wife, telling her how sorry you are about all the people talking about her in town. Sorry for how difficult it would be for her to carry on and face the people at work. Then go on and write a letter to your son and tell him how sorry you are for his pain of not having a dad around and having to go to school every day being known as the kid whose father killed himself.

So if you ever find yourself feeling down, reach out for some help and start with the people you love.

Enough about the sad talk! Let's have some fun and get back to the tattoos. I know a guy in his sixties who had a grim reaper tattooed on his chest when he was in his twenties. Now that he has aged and his body is not as fit as it once was, that grim reaper looks like Yoda from Star Wars. Another friend of ours had a Chinese symbol tattooed on her arm. She said it means peace and love, but since she does not read Chinese, for all she knows it could say "Number seven combination with an egg roll."

My youngest brother got a tattoo in remembrance of his best friend who died in a car accident. This is a perfect example of making a decision on an emotional impulse without much thought for the future or the consequences. He has been embarrassed about it for years and is now looking into having it removed.

He also has to explain to his young son why he has those marks on his body.

My advice would be if you are thinking of getting a tattoo, get a fake one for a few weeks and see if you still think it is cool.

"When one door closes, another opens; but we often look so long and so regretfully upon the closed door that we do not see the one which has opened for us."
— Alexander Graham Bell, Inventor of the telephone

Chapter Twenty-Six
Self-Esteem

What is Self-Esteem?

Self-esteem is simply what you think of yourself. People with high self-esteem believe in their hearts that they deserve to be happy, that they have the right to stand up for their needs. They have trust in their abilities to deal with problems that come up in life.

People with low self-esteem on the other hand, believe that they don't have the right or even the ability to stand up for themselves. Although I learned from having low self esteem that there are cracks in the foundation everywhere you go, no one is perfect. When you hang your head low for so long, you can see imperfections everywhere, even in multi-billion dollar airports like Toronto, Ontario or Phoenix, Arizona. They look beautiful at a glance, but if you take a look at the beautiful granite floors, there are cracks everywhere. This reminds me that we all have little cracks in our own foundations.

How can you raise your self-esteem?

You can get an almost certain self-esteem boost by putting into practice the following suggestions below. This will give you a more clear sense of who you are and will raise your self-esteem.

Six ways to raise your self-esteem

1. Don't deny or lie about a problem (even to yourself). Whenever you are confronted with a problem in life, no matter how unpleasant, rather than burying your head in the sand, confront the problem head on. Admit the truth, no matter how painful it may be, and search for ways to solve the problem. There is a way.

2. Get up and do something. The person who lays in bed or on the couch everyday never feels as good about himself or herself as someone who is always participating in things. Human beings were not meant to vegetate. We were meant to engage in goal-oriented behavior. So start with small things, such as getting up and cleaning the house. Answer the mail. Make that annoying phone call to check on something you ordered. When you accomplish something, you feel much better about yourself than when you sit and do nothing.

3. Succeed in something, no matter how small. The feeling of being successful and capable builds self-esteem. When you take on a challenge and overcome it, you feel better about yourself. Start with a small success that will help in your daily life. For example, I know many people who type very slowly on the computer keyboard when a simple typing course would improve their speed. How great these people would feel if they called their local business school and took a course. Soon they would accomplish something that would remind them on a daily basis that they had taken action. I did this myself. Christine had me take a typing course and before long I was typing much better and feeling great about myself.

4. Absolutely, positively change your negative thinking. When you make a mistake in front of people, do you put yourself down? Maybe this habit started when you were a child, and your parents called you a dummy every time you made a mistake. Every time you catch yourself saying something like, "I am so stupid, what is wrong with me?" Instead say "Whoops, I made a mistake. I guess I'm human." Believe it or not, even that simple change will go a long way in building your self-esteem. In time, you

will stop condemning yourself every time you make a mistake, and instead you will forgive yourself, and give yourself some room to be human. You learn by making mistakes.

5. Don't say "Yes" when you want to say "No". If you always say yes, then your no will have no meaning. This was a big one for me because I would often feel guilty when saying no. Your self-esteem suffers when you don't assert yourself. This happens when you go along with something because you feel too embarrassed or too intimidated to take a stand and speak up about what you really want in life. In life we often find ourselves saying yes when we should say no simply because of our strong desire to be loved and accepted by others. So the next time you find yourself about to say "Yes" when you really mean "NO", stop dead in your tracks. Say, "No" and let the other person deal with it. Your self–esteem and sense of your own power will grow each time you do it. And the other person will respect you for that decision. My good friend Adam Carroll says "In life when you make hard decisions, life becomes easy and when you make easy decisions, life becomes hard."

6. Don't give up your dream—this is the key to high self-esteem. This is one of the most important factors in building self-esteem. If you give up your dream, it is very hard to have a high self-esteem. How can you respect yourself if you feel as if you have sold out? Never give up hope that you will someday be able to correct your course in life. Don't give up. If you keep focused on achieving your goals your self-esteem will rise. You will feel good about yourself because you have not abandoned yourself or your dreams.

*"Your chances of success in any undertaking can always be
measured by your belief in yourself."*
— Robert Collier

Chapter Twenty-Seven
Healthy Habits

Run Forrest, Run! No thank you, I'll walk...

The only exercise I was getting for quite a while were mood swings! I had a $300 exercise bike that looked like a clothesline because I just used it for hanging towels and t-shirts. It took me a long time to realize that diet and exercise are two very important solvents for the brain. They also helped immensely in overcoming depression.

I am not talking about getting up and running a marathon, although my good friends Myra and Antonio run several a year and are full of energy daily. Walking is just as good for your mind and body as any other exercise. And if you're in a wheelchair, you can still get moving. Remember "No matter how slow you go you are still faster everybody sitting on the couch."

Here are some facts about walking:

- Walking improves memory. People in tests who walked on a treadmill were better at correctly identifying which numbers were repeated in a series of digits read aloud.
- Walking also improves attention, improving your ability to ignore distractions. Probably because walking activates the brain regions associated with attention.
- Biking and running may get your heart racing, but a low intensity stroll down your street five to six times a week is actually more effective in preventing obesity and eliminating heart risk factors including high cholesterol and blood pressure.
- Walkers trim their waistlines more and shed more

weight. This will also make you feel great.

My family doctor shared with me that if I exercised regularly, it would sharpen my mind, relieve stress and improve my life overall by increasing my energy levels. At first I just shrugged it off. I wanted to learn how to speak better, read better and do simple math. But then I thought, what the heck and gave it a try. I started walking ten to fifteen minutes before my speech therapy appointment and to my amazement I started making progress in a short period of time.

I found that I was more alert, relaxed and able to focus on what I was doing. I felt that regular walking helped me greatly with my depression and anxiety. It lowered my tension and sadness and improved my overall mood. So much so that I was able to wean myself off all medication within one year. Before you do this, please consult your doctor. And realize that for these effects to be long term, you must maintain a regular and consistent schedule of exercise along with a good diet.

Walking regularly has also boosted my self-confidence and energy levels. After a while you will begin to see the positive results that come from regular exercise and you will feel good about yourself when you lower your daily stress level and decrease your feeling of anxiety in daily living. So the next time you feel yourself getting stressed or upset, lace up your shoes and take a walk around the block. If you are in a wheelchair, wheel yourself around the block and come home feeling refreshed.

I know it is hard to get started and easy to say, "Maybe tomorrow I will start walking". I often reminded myself that I said tomorrow, yesterday! Would it be worth ten minutes of your time to start a lifetime of change? Start right now, set the book down and go for a ten minute walk and see how you feel when you get back. I guarantee you'll feel great.

Walking is just one way to increase your energy levels. For the longest time I didn't realize the connection between success in recovery and my level of energy. Just for a minute, stop and think about someone you know who is successful in life or who has had a successful recovery and you will probably discover that they are full of energy. They have the energy to keep going and going even when there are obstacles in their way.

I would like to briefly go over some things you can do in life to increase your energy. I know it can be very difficult to believe you can muster up the energy to do something, especially if you're suffering from depression, laying in bed for hours a day staring at the ceiling just wishing everything would go away. That type of lifestyle drains you of your precious energy.

On the following pages are some ideas that may help you to regain your energy and believe me, you will just have to make the effort to try some of these and see for yourself how much your life can improve.

Sleep

I know I just said in the last paragraph that it is not good for you to lie in bed all day, but good sleep is an important part of increasing your energy. When you are sleeping, you are in repair. Your mind, muscles and entire body is repairing itself while you sleep so it is very important to get a good sleep every night. Some things that may help you sleep better include keeping your room dark and quiet. If you have streetlights outside your bedroom window you could hang up dark curtains or a blanket over the window. It is also helpful to turn off all radios and televisions because it is hard to get full rest when your brain is occupied by the noise of the television or radio. Try to get eight hours of sleep a night. It may seem impossible but you can try. I also rest during the day when I am feeling tired, often a twenty minute nap will recharge my batteries.

Diet

This is very important for your energy levels. I'm not going to preach for you to become a vegetarian or eat certain foods, you can eat whatever you want. For myself I found that my energy levels would rise when I ate a lot of fruits and vegetables. They are far easier for your body to digest, using less energy than if you eat a greasy hamburger. What usually happens after eating a Christmas or Thanksgiving dinner? You usually see a lot of people hitting the couch because they feel drained. Their bodies are using up a lot of energy to digest all that food and is all that food good for us? Turkey, mashed potatoes, gravy, stuffing, buns with butter, cakes. You get the idea and it's up to you to decide what you want to put into your energy gas tank: premium fuel or the cheap brand.

Organization

You may wonder how being organized can boost your energy and I wondered the same thing myself. I learned this simple technique from my occupational therapists, Gary and Claudia. For a long time I was disorganized. I would let things slide because I didn't care about them and then I would become frustrated because I couldn't find things. This became very emotionally draining and consumed a lot of my energy. Eventually they set me up on a routine to organize and clean my house and office. Once I was able to make this habit, it was very easy to keep on top of it. It also boosted my self-esteem and energy levels by knowing where everything was located. I was no longer wasting precious time and energy looking for things. I also found that with a clear desk came a clear mind.

Lower your caffeine intake

I used to be a coffee junkie, some days drinking 10 to 12 cups a day. Don't get me wrong, I still love coffee but I limit it to 2 to 3 cups a day and no longer drink any after 11 a.m. I also no longer drink pop or other soft drinks that contain caffeine, especially those energy drinks (stay away). They will rob you of your energy in the long run. I can't guarantee this will work for you but I feel great and if you want to try it, it doesn't cost a thing.

"In every person that comes near you, look for what is good and strong; honor that; try to imitate it, and your faults will drop off like dead leaves when their time comes." — John Ruskin, English Philosopher

H20
Water: The World's first energy drink.

There are some facts about water that I want to bring up. I know a lot about water because I have researched its properties and benefits to the human body.

Water is very important to the brain.

The average human brain is seventy to seventy-eight per cent water, so if you neglect drinking water you can imagine what it does to your brain. It would be like driving from New York to Daytona Beach on one tank of gas. Eventually you'll find yourself on the side of the road wondering what happened. Drinking coffee, cola and alcohol is not the same as drinking water. Caffeine in colas and coffee actually dehydrate you. Alcohol also does the same thing, it keeps you wanting more. When you drink a cold beer on a hot day you want another and another.

So take a break in between those drinks and have a glass of water. You will feel better and it will cost you less money.

Water facts:
Here are some other facts that you may be interested to know about water;

When brain cells have a sufficient amount of drinking

water they are able to circulate fresh oxygen-laden blood freely through the brain. This allows the brain to remain fresh and alert. Even a small decrease in the amount of water you drink every day can make a difference in your brain's performance. It can actually drop your brain performance as much as twenty to thirty percent.

Water keeps your eyes and mouth moist; it washes dirt and dust away from your eyes and lubricates your mouth, which is important when trying to speak. When you are learning to speak again, it is easier with a wet whistle than a dry pasty one.

Our bodies use drinking water to digest food in our stomach. A lack of water will slow the process of digestion, which may also lead to constipation or other discomforts.

Your muscles are able to work longer without tiring. As long as you have a good supply of drinking water that supplies oxygen to your muscles, you will be hydrated, which is very important especially in hot weather.

Speaking of hot weather, your body temperature is maintained through the use of water. The water regulates your body temperature through sweat when it's hot. Sweat cools the body, but sweat uses up your water supply. This is just another reason to drink plenty of water. Two litres of water per day is recommended for hydration.

Your nerve cells transmit messages to and from the brain. To do this they use electrolytes. Drinking water is an important way to maintain electrolytes at such a level that your nerves can do their work.

Your kidneys filter waste, which leaves your body in the form of urine which is almost entirely water, so you must constantly replace that water to avoid a build up of toxins in the body that may make you sick.

Stay away from the high sugar, high caffeine energy drinks; they will do you more harm than good.

"Resentment is like drinking poison and then hoping it will kill your enemies."
— *Nelson Mandela, Winner of the Nobel Peace Prize*

Chapter Twenty-Eight

Anger

Anger is the cloud that hides the sun

Anger will either slow down or completely stop the recovery process. It is hard enough learning new things with a brain injury; it is even more difficult when you are angry or upset about something.

If you are bit by a snake it is not the bite that will kill you, it is the venom streaming through your body. Anger is like venom and the way to remove it is with forgiveness.

Think about a time when you were at work or school and couldn't focus because you were angry with someone from an argument the night before. You may just nod your head instead of paying attention because you are thinking about how to get even with that person. This drains so much energy from you. Energy you could put towards learning new things. So when someone or something makes you angry or does you wrong, you have some choices: you can talk about it and straighten out the situation immediately, you can change the way you think about it, or you can simply let it go.

"What, let it go? But I can't let it go!" That is probably the hardest thing to do for most people because there is a feeling of wanting revenge.

I will get even. Getting even is a form of self-pity; it is a virus that will drag you down very fast to a place where no one wants to be. You may think, "They will never say that to me again". Well that may make you feel better for a little while but if you reflect on your life, there are probably things you wish you had let go, because now you don't talk to the person or you feel very uncomfortable in their company. You avoid them on the street and think to yourself, "If I would have let that go, I wouldn't feel this way right now".

So the next time you run into a difficult situation, stop and think before you react or speak. That simple pause, thinking about how you will react, can reduce a lot of stress and anxiety in the future. Your response to the event will determine the outcome, so unless someone backs over your new car with a bulldozer on purpose, try to let things go. If someone really does something bad to you, it might be a good idea to part ways and have nothing to do with them at all. I was angry for a few years after coming home from the hospital. Angry at the driver for talking on his cell phone, angry at the fire department for getting me out of the car, angry with myself for now being such a burden on my family and friends. All of this anger created a massive energy drain and really made me tired. When you are tired something as little as a person chewing gum too loud can tick you off!

Remember this; anger is created by YOU and YOU alone. Not your family, not your friends, not the doctors that told you that you might be better in a few months and you're angry because it has not happened yet. You control how you respond to the things that come your way. I'm not saying to keep everything bottled up like a volcano ready to explode at the first thing you see. Sometimes it is good to get things off your chest, to vent your anger and frustration, so you can say, "That feels better".

Getting angry for a short time is a lot easier than brewing up a long costly plan to get even. That is like trying to pour more water into a glass that is already full, you just make a mess.

You must first empty the glass by expressing your feelings and concerns to make room for more. First let others do the same. Listen to them and let them express their hopes and dreams, fears and concerns, hurts and pains, before you talk about yours. It opens up a space inside of them to be able to listen and take in what you have to say. When you channel those energies into helping yourself and others, you are on the road to success and your success is the ultimate payback, not revenge.

Four categories that trigger our anger

1. We become angry when someone demeans or attacks our self-esteem.
2. We become angry when someone or something prevents us from reaching a significant goal that we believe is rightfully ours.
3. We become angry when someone or something violates our basic principles or values, such as fair play or honesty. (Someone who cheats when you play golf. I am not going to mention any names ...)
4. We become angry when we feel helpless to correct a "wrong" in our lives or to fix a situation that has gone bad.

Behind your anger there is hope

Here are some tips for overcoming anger that I have used myself to get out of this dark cloud. It is good to know that behind our anger is hope. Hope for something better. If you get angry because something in your life is not going the way you would like it to, then that is a signal telling you to change things. Ask yourself, "What would I rather be experiencing right now?" Then go ahead and make those changes.

-   Getting to know your early warning signs will give you a heads-up for what is to come. I have learned to know myself inside and out so that I can detect the early warning signs of anger. We all have them, some are different than others but either way they're sending your body a signal. I would start to feel symptoms of a hot face. I could feel it burning, I would clench my teeth together, tighten my fists and I could feel my heart racing. These symptoms then became my signal to step back, take a deep breath and think about the situation. For example a driver would cut me off in traffic and give me the middle finger. Something so little would set me off in a rage. The reason was, I took it personally. I didn't know what was going on in that person's life. Maybe his wife just left him or his dog just died. I stopped wasting my time trying to figure out why people in this world are mean to each other because that is a waste of time and energy. It is none of my business what other people think of me. Treat people the way you want to be treated.

- Reason with yourself, become an expert on yourself, keep an anger diary - the triggers, frequency and intensity. Is there a pattern? Are there particular people or irritating situations? My dad's first wife was killed by a train when her vehicle was hit at a crossing. Growing up I remember him getting angry everytime he would hear or see a train. Begin to reason with yourself. Is it worth it? Are you justified?

- Practice thought stopping. Think of a word you can say aloud to trigger your brain. By interrupting your thought pattern, you can stop the negative thoughts into your head. A friend shared with me that his signal is 'lights on, lights off.' Using those simple words, he can shut off the negative thoughts just as easy as a light switch and leave those angry thoughts in the dark where they should be.

- Avoid overstimulation. Care for yourself through nutrition, rest and exercise. Take care of your physical well-being as well as your mental health.

- Practice effective communication. Don't beat around the bush. Many people become angry because they take things the wrong way. Say what you mean and mean what you say.

- Practice empathy. See life through someone else's eyes. Just like the guy who cut me off in traffic, maybe he's also going through a bad time in his life.

- Practice tolerance. Accept people as they are, and not as you would like them to be. Have fewer rules about how you expect people around you to behave and live their lives.
- Practice forgiveness. Wipe your chalkboard clear so to speak, just let it go.
- Practice relaxation. Find a quiet area where you can take some deep breaths and relax.
- Laugh at yourself.
- Practice meditation. I have been meditating daily for years now and have no remaining feelings of anger.

Give up all blaming and complaining. This was a big step for me with amazing results. You see most of the time we are blaming and complaining, it is to the wrong person. I would go to work and complain about my wife and then go home at night and complain to my wife about the people at work. Neither one of them could do anything about what I was complaining about. I had to learn to face issues head on. If I'm not happy with someone or something, I will tell the person directly now. For so many years I would get angry over silly things that I thought should be a certain way and then blame other people when things didn't go that way. When we blame and complain we have a reference point of something better that we want and we are not willing to risk doing what is necessary to achieve it.

Much of my anger was created by the expectations I had of how the world should be, but wasn't. Once I was able to let go of those expectations I stopped creating new anger. For me this was a huge shift in my life, not only emotionally but physically as well. I also felt better and had more energy. Many of my aches and pains that I had carried around for years were gone, and best of all I rarely get headaches.

Stop focusing on anger because what you focus on will

increase. It is much better to focus on peace and gratitude and you will bring more of that into your life.

As you can see, there are four things that make people angry, but there are far more ways to not to be angry.

Chapter Twenty-Nine

Laughter

"Forrest is doing well, but we need to keep
him for a few more days because
I'm lonely and he's funny."

**"Dear funny bone, I miss you dearly. When this cast
comes off of my arm, I hope you are still there"**

For years I denied myself the one thing that would
eventually be one of the keys to unlock my shackles of
depression and anxiety, and that was laughter. I don't know
why I denied myself laughter. Sometimes when I would laugh,
I would feel guilty and think the worst. Maybe the doctors
and therapists would think I wasn't taking my recovery
seriously. I really don't know why. Maybe because brain
injury and depression is not something to laugh at, I don't
know. But lucky for me I realized that laughter is the best
medicine (Unless of course you have a stomach infection,
then penicillin works better).

Once you learn to laugh and to laugh at yourself, you can
truly begin to heal inside and out. It was a couple of years
after the accident before I had a good laugh, a very good one.
You know the kind when your stomach hurts and your eyes
begin to water. Wow!

I thought "I haven't felt like this since I was a kid!" It was euphoria. From then on I thought, "This can't be wrong, it feels so good." So I made sure that I would laugh and smile every day. I watched funny television shows and funny movies, anything that was a comedy and made me feel better. The force that propels human action is emotions and feelings. If you love what you're doing it is much easier to do it. And if you can have a laugh at the same time, even better.

This goes for speech therapy, occupational therapy and all the other therapies out there. If the person has no interest or personal connection to the project, they will have no motivation to complete the task. In therapy there must be a way for the person to personalize each project they are working on, even in the slightest way. It might just be the spark to ignite that person to get motivated to be well and to help themselves heal.

Laughter increases endorphin levels

Endorphins are tiny chemicals in the brain that reduce pain and anxiety and increase the feeling of well-being. They also stimulate the immune system. Some of the other events in our life that release endorphins are eating chocolate, sunbathing, exercising and falling in love. All of these things will make a person feel good. If you want someone to fall in love with you, feed them chocolate on an exercise bike on a sunny day. Take a few minutes out of your day and find something to laugh and smile about.

Here are some facts about laughter and smiling:

- Women smile more than men.
- It takes only seventeen muscles to smile compared to forty-three muscles to frown.
- A smile is a universal expression of happiness and is recognized as such by all cultures so even if you are unable to speak at this point, just smile. It will make

you feel good as well as others around you.

- A smiling person is judged to be more pleasant, attractive, sincere, sociable and competent.
- Happy people generally don't get sick as often as people who are unhappy.
- People are born with the ability to smile. Even babies, who are born blind, smile.
- Generally, adults laugh approximately fifteen times per day, while children laugh around four hundred times a day.
- People who smile often will live longer.
- Laughter needs no translation.
- In clinical tests laughter has proven to be more than three times more effective than morphine to reduce pain.

Try this little test today

Smile at everyone you see, and laugh often. At the end of the day, notice how you feel and whether people acted differently around you.

It took some practice for me to do this, but what I did was stand in front of a mirror every morning for about five minutes with a huge grin on my face. The smile led to laughter and throughout the day I couldn't stop giggling every time I thought of myself standing in front of the mirror. Try it for yourself. I know it sounds goofy but it works.

Happiness leads to smiling and smiling leads to happiness. Happiness is your natural immunity, having a positive effect on your health and well-being. If you don't feel like smiling, smile anyway. It's a start.

Take this 90 day free trial of smiling and laughing and then decide if you want to return to the old miserable you or if you enjoy being happy. Then keep it up for the rest of your life and share it with everyone.

"I will never understand all the good that a simple smile can accomplish."
— Mother Teresa

Chapter Thirty
Marriage

In marriage it is important to treat all of your disasters as incidents and none of your incidents as disasters.

One thing that has to be said up front about being married to the person with acquired brain injury is: Do not be angry with your wife or husband for what has happened to you. They did not create the state you are in. It is not their fault for what is going on in your life. Realize that if they are there with you, they obviously love you. So don't push them away and they will then give you the same in return.

If you feel that you're getting angry and going to fight, lay down on the couch for a few minutes. I find it is very difficult to be angry when I'm lying down. It may sound silly but try it. You may also find it helpful to go back to the anger section of this book and review a few strategies for overcoming anger.

One thing you can do if you are the spouse of a survivor and tensions are heating up, is to take a time out. My wife used to do this with me. When an argument started she would say "Give me a minute to think about this". What this did was cause a delay and it gave us time to clear the air and defuse the situation. Most of the time I didn't even realize it had happened. If you can't speak, use the 'T' symbol with your hands like a referee does at a football game meaning 'time out'.

The other option you have is to keep yelling at your partner and the next thing you know you'll find yourself alone and the only one you will have to yell at is yourself in a very lonely house. Please keep this in mind. I have seen it happen to too many people and it would be nice to prevent others from doing the same just by reading and understanding this section of the book. I can't say it any more clearly: treat your spouse with disrespect and you'll find yourself alone without a spouse.

Statistics say that only one in twenty couples will stay married after one of the partners receives a brain injury. Wow! That is only five percent. A lot of people I have met with brain injuries will say "My partner is not the same person I married". Well, perhaps that's true. With your help and support, perhaps they will be a better person than before. Remember "For better or worse."

I understand how frustrating it must be for a husband or wife living with someone with a brain injury and it is compounded even more when you add children and depression into the picture. If you truly care for that person, try to stick it out through the good times and the bad. It takes time to recover from this, lots of time. It is also the time when the person needs you the most. You wouldn't plant a seed in the ground and come back the next day looking at the ground feeling disappointed because the plant hasn't sprouted yet. Don't expect your partner to be the same as before the injury just after a few months of rehabilitation. Plant the seed and have patience; nurture it and you will watch your relationship grow into something wonderful.

Remember, it is okay to say "I don't know", or "Please help me with this." Being humble goes a long way. Recognize the fact that your partner has the right to be different, and that they are not you. Finally, remember your partner is not the clay and you are not the potter so don't try to mold them into what you want. Let me ask you this, have you ever wanted someone to change? And did they change because you wanted them to? Probably not.

Practice a little "live and let live". Most people I have met dislike being told "You're wrong". You have a right to your own opinion and sometimes it is better to keep it to yourself.

Sure there are times when I thought of packing it in, and just saying "To hell with this. I don't need this crap. I'm out of here." But they were only thoughts. Once I cooled down I would think things over and realize things would not be better somewhere else. I knew that my problems would just come with me wherever I went, so it was up to me to change my thoughts and my attitude. I have been married now twenty years. Over half of that time, I have been living with a brain injury and so have my wife and son. So as time goes by, things do get better. In the beginning it is a rough and rocky road and yes it does suck!

But know this, if you work at it everything improves slowly but surely. Small changes over time become a massive change.

Remember, if you are not loved, nothing else matters, not the car you drive, the house you live in, nothing.

In volunteering at a retirement home, I have met many interesting people. Max and Eva have been married for sixty-seven years, so I thought if I want advice on how to keep a marriage together, these would be the people to ask. I interviewed them for this book, and simply asked what is their secret to a long marriage. They said there was no secret. Their method was in fact very simple.

Here are a few of the points they made to me:

- Never go to bed angry at each other, this will also help you sleep better.
- They walk together every day. Fresh air is the key, even if it is only ten minutes after supper in a snowstorm. Make time! You don't even have to talk to each other on the walk, just enjoy the scenery and time together.
- They said watch your pennies and to spend less than

you make. Most marriage failures that they have seen over the years ended because of financial problems. They say to talk about your finances together and only make large purchases together.

- Let things go. Ask yourself before you get angry, "Is this really important?" Forgive.
- Have a sense of humor. Most of life's troubles don't seem so big if you can both have a laugh about it.
- Rest every day, even if it is only for ten or fifteen minutes. It will recharge your batteries and leave you with a better outlook on things.
- Never let your marriage turn into a two-headed coin, that's when you're stuck together but you can't face each other. Find a way to work things out.

Chapter Thirty-One
Safety and Problems with Attention

Looking back now, my wife can tell me what an average day was like after I came home from the hospital. I needed to be constantly reminded to stay focused on what I was doing. My friends gave me the nickname "Ping", because I was like a ping-pong ball bouncing back and forth, back and forth. I was all over the place but not getting anything done.

One day while brushing my teeth, I looked out the window and thought "Hey, the bird feeder is empty", so I put my toothbrush down and went outside to fill the bird feeder. Only later did I realize that I had not finished brushing my teeth, shaving or combing my hair. To the outside world it would look like I was lazy or I didn't care about myself anymore but really it was neither. Had I forgotten to do the simple things in the morning? Or was I just distracted?

Many things like background noise or a change of scenery easily distracted me. This went on for a few years until I was able to focus clearly on each task I was doing. It is hard to focus on any one thing for a period of time. Once you learn to focus, you will be surprised by how much more you can accomplish in life.

Your mind works the same way as a magnifying glass with the sun behind you. If you focus the magnifying glass long enough on a piece of paper, it will catch fire every time. But if you move the magnifying glass around, nothing will happen and you're just wasting your time.

In order to prevent accidents around the house and in the work place, you can focus on one thing at a time, such as:

Cooking
If you are cooking, stay in the kitchen and watch the stove

until your meal is complete. The old saying goes "A watched pot never boils". Believe me it does, even more if you don't watch it. If you go into the other room to watch the television you could start a fire. I know because I've done this.

Children

Know your limitations especially with children in your care, I accidentally left the house while my son was sleeping alone, and let me tell you this caused a lot of friction with the whole family.

Tools

If you are working with tools, be aware of your surroundings and focus on what you are doing. Otherwise you could injure yourself just like I have done it many times. It is not a good thing when the emergency room staff know you by your first name.

These statements may seem very basic and obvious to most people. But to the person with a brain injury, sometimes all it takes is a phone to ring or the doorbell to go off and you can immediately forget what you were doing.

When you slow down and focus on what you are doing, you will get more done. You must complete each task to the end and make this a habit. Once this becomes a routine the speed will follow.

Just like the magnifying glass, if you move around from task to task, nothing will get accomplished. No job will be complete and you will become overwhelmed with the backlog in your life. So once again, you have to focus.

I know what it is like to want to prove to everyone and to yourself that you're as good as you used to be. Well, you may not be. So take a step back and know your limitations. If you re-learn your skills safely, you may be able to do the things you used to. But if you go out and hurt yourself or someone else, this will create doubt in yourself and others about your abilities and it will slow down your recovery process. No job has priority over safety.

"Happiness does not depend on outward things, but on the way we see them."
— *Leo Tolstoy, Novelist and Philosopher*

Chapter Thirty-Two

The Company Party Theory

For friends and family to understand how difficult it is for a person with an acquired brain injury to pay attention in everyday situations, I will try to explain it like your company party.

You are engaged in a conversation at the party when suddenly you hear your name mentioned in a nearby conversation. You turn your attention to the conversation where you heard your name, and suddenly you can no longer hear the original conversation.

This occurs because your brain cannot process two conversations at one time. With an acquired brain injury, it may not be another conversation in the room but a radio or television that is the distraction. When possible, pay attention to your surroundings and background noise. It will be much easier to get your message across.

So many times I would nod my head as if I understood what people were saying, but in reality I was distracted by something and didn't understand.

"If you put a small value on yourself, rest assured that the world will not raise your price."
— Anonymous

Chapter Thirty-Three
The Power of Three

I remember the first time I saw my friend Chad. I was at a brain injury conference and was mesmerized by his infectious smile. I immediately liked him and I didn't even know his name yet.

I wanted to have his outlook and thought to myself, how can someone who has gone through a life changing brain injury be so happy and positive? His secret was helping others. He told me he volunteers and coaches kids. If it worked for him, could it possibly work for me? Well, fast forward several years and yes, it does work and I love it. I volunteer at a local retirement home and make it a habit to do three nice things a day; one for myself, one for my family and one for a stranger. I call it the power of three. The power of three has brought so much into my life. I really want for nothing else than to give more.

It works the same way as the most powerful tool in the world, Compound interest. The way compound interest works is this: you put a little money away every week or month in your bank account and don't touch it. For a few years you probably won't see much of a change while it grows very slowly. Eventually you'll see an explosive growth. Your money will double and if you leave it long enough it will double again and so on. That little amount that you put in at the beginning has now turned into super numbers. Well, if you do a minimum of three nice things a day, you will be rewarded with compound interest in the form of joy, love, confidence, opportunities, success and many other things just by knowing that you helped so many people in their lives. There are many other people that will love the chance to give back to you in any way they can.

When you do something nice for someone, not only

would they love to give back to you, but also their family and friends. This is where the fifty dollars a week turns into one million dollars by virtue of compound interest. Just imagine if you did three nice things a day for one year. That is over one thousand good deeds. Can you imagine how different your life would be if one thousand good things happened to you throughout a year?

This practice has made massive changes in my life. So take an interest in people and invest some time and before you know it, you'll be rich in many ways. Doing these nice things can be as simple as holding doors open, putting your dishes away, looking a stranger in the eye, or talking to someone who's in a wheelchair. Smile and say hello. This is a big one for me because I was in a wheelchair for a few months. I also have many good friends in wheelchairs and I wouldn't trade that time for all the money in the world. I learned so much about society and myself. For some reason people don't make a lot of eye contact when you are in a wheelchair. I would like to change that by sharing with as many people as I can that a person in a chair is no different than you or I, and that everyone has a sense of humor and feelings. We are all human, there is no difference. The next time you meet a person in a wheelchair, treat them with the same respect as the person standing beside you. Please.

Other possibilities include helping a neighbor cut their grass or shovel their snow. Help someone learn to read or write. There are a million nice things to do and millions of rewards for doing them. The first and greatest reward is feeling good about yourself. It is a great confidence builder for both you and the person you help. Chad and I have become good friends and we both continue to do what we can to help other people.

> *"Confidence is contagious; so is the lack of it."*
> *— Anonymous*

Chapter Thirty-Four
The Face of an Angel

"I kissed the face of an angel, but I didn't get to say goodbye"

Volunteering is a big part of the recovery process. One of my doctors said it would help me get back to being around people and really help with my social skills. At first I tried volunteering at my son's school doing lunch duty monitoring, I have to admit that didn't last long. I couldn't handle 300 kids running and screaming, it was just too overwhelming. I thought of volunteering at the hospital to give back to the people who helped me. My doctor thought it may be too soon because of the depression I was going through. It could have been difficult for me to see more people going through the same thing. My occupational therapist said she had a friend who ran the recreational activities at a local retirement lodge, so off I went.

I have to admit my first day there was very intimidating, but to my surprise it was not at all what I expected. I was introduced as the new volunteer for recreational activities, such as cards and shuffleboard. The first woman I met there was Margaret. She was an angel. She came up and gave me a big hug and said "Welcome aboard!" Margaret was full of vim, vigor and vitality. She was fun loving and carefree and always had a big hug and kiss for me and my son whom I brought with me every week. She always had funny sayings like "Family is like fudge, sweet with a few nuts." The nice thing about Margaret and all the other people there was that they didn't care what I drove, how I dressed, whether I had forgotten to comb my hair or if I stuttered. As it turns out they wanted the same thing as me: love, acceptance and companionship. That wasn't very hard to give and believe me it wasn't hard to get back in return. Margaret and my son Hunter had a little secret. She would sneak him into the kitchen and give him cookies. She was a real sweetheart.

One week after Christmas, Hunter and I returned for shuffleboard as always on Tuesday night. We were knocking on doors up and down the halls to round up all the regular players when we noticed Margaret's room was empty. She had passed away just after Christmas. That was a real heartbreaker for both of us and it was then that I realized I had kissed the face of an angel, but I didn't get to say goodbye.

Everybody in the world is so busy with their lives and we forget that life will one day end. And we don't know when that day will be. Before it's too late please tell everyone you care for, how much you love them, and how important they are to you. I hope you find a Margaret in your life. I hope you find an angel.

People who know me know that I love to give hugs to everyone. This is important in my life. It not only makes me feel good, but I believe it makes the other people feel good too. I believe that a hug from someone can do more for you in life than any pill or medical device out there. A hug can raise your spirits when you're feeling low and skyrocket them when you're feeling good. Go ahead and try it for a week and I bet that you will keep on doing it for life.

One thing Margaret said that stuck in my head was, "Relax and take a turtle for a walk." At first I did not understand what she was talking about but now I do. It may seem silly but I did take a turtle for a walk. By that I mean I walked down my road very, very slowly just like a turtle and noticed so many things that I hadn't noticed before, like the bees on a flower, the sound of the wind blowing through the leaves and all the other things we take for granted as we rush along in our busy lives. I hope you can find it in yourself to take a turtle for a walk. You will discover all of these different little things that are very calming and you will also see many of your worries going away, at least for a little while.

> *"Example is not the main thing influencing others.*
> *It is the only thing."*
> — *Albert Schweitzer, Medical missionary*

Chapter Thirty-Five
Get Rid of the BMW's

Bitchers, Moaners and Whiners

Have you ever made progress in your recovery listening to others bitch about how bad they have it? No? So why do it? If you are the person bitching and moaning, please stop now. You're only digging yourself into a hole and no one wants to be with you. If you ever find yourself in that hole, stop digging!

If you don't believe me, look around you. Are there less people phoning you? Has the number of people coming to visit you decreased? These may well be signals that you are turning into a negative person that no one wants to be around. And the signals are everywhere. You just have to open your eyes to see them.

Perhaps your girlfriend or boyfriend keeps cancelling their date with you or the guys from work don't ask you to join them for a get together on the weekend. Believe me, it's not because you have a brain injury or depression. So you can give up the victim mentality, it's because of the way you are acting. Sometimes people think that they can get more attention if they act out in anger. This may be true but is this really the type of attention you want?

I was recently in my physiotherapist's office and a mother pushed her teenage boy in a wheelchair into the room. It was clear he had a broken leg and looked uncomfortable and while we were in the waiting room all he did was bitch at his mother. "How come it takes so long? This place sucks, I'm tired of this crap, and I shouldn't have to wait." I felt so bad for the mother. You could tell she was so embarrassed. This young man needed a lesson in manners. He also needed to realize that his mother was his caregiver. The word is very self-explanatory.

"Caregiver". That's what they do, they care for you. And you want to treat them like a piece of garbage? It is no wonder why so many families break up and people get divorced after something tragic happens to a family member.

My advice to the person with an injury is to think before you speak and ask yourself, "Is this really important?" Everyone has to wait in line. You too. So just take a deep breath and relax. The person that brought you there did so because they love you. So why would you want to act out in a manner that would drive that person away from you?

The next time you're in a situation like that and you want to speak up and be heard by everyone in the waiting room or pharmacy, tell them some good news. That is guaranteed to get people's attention. Good news does more than get attention. Good news pleases people and helps them relax. You could say things like, "This is my fourteenth time in physiotherapy and I feel much better than I did when I first came. This place is great and the people make you feel welcome!"

That is something positive that will create interest from other people in the waiting room. Telling them how far you've come will be an inspiration to everyone there rather than telling them how bad things are.

Now you might be able to see how you can get the same point across and be positive and attract people to you instead of having people push away from you. Remember to respect and love your caregivers who are always there for you. I realize that when you are angry, the easiest ones to hurt are the ones that love you and are closest to you. I don't know why that is.

I've done it many times myself and now wish I could take

it all back after seeing how many people I hurt with my anger. I hope the pages in this book will allow you to avoid a lot of the pain and anguish that I went through, and that I put my family through. Once again, before you burst out with your bitching and whining because little Jimmy spilled juice on the table just ask yourself, "Is this really important"? When you ask that question it gives you a moment to think rather than reacting immediately. It has helped me in many situations so possibly write that point down and stick it on your fridge until it becomes a habit.

Chapter Thirty-Six
Caregiver Burnout Trap

Don't fall into the Trap of 'Caregiver Burnout'
At the time of writing this I have been visiting two close friends in the hospital, neither one with a brain injury. As time passes, I can see the toll it takes on the caregiver because they want to be at the hospital for every moment. I have spent quite a bit of time with each of the caregivers of these friends, explaining the dangers of making themselves sick both physically and emotionally if they don't take care of themselves. And if this happens they won't be able to take care of their loved one when they need them the most.

Caring for a person with an acquired brain injury requires quite a bit of your time and energy. Yes, it can be a very rewarding experience. But it can also be demanding and stressful, taking a lot out of you physically and emotionally. If you see any of the following ten signs of stress overwhelming yourself or someone you care about please take action and get some help.

- Denial about the injury and the future effects it will have on the person with the injury. "Don't worry; Forrest is going to be fine, there is nothing wrong. Everyone is just over-reacting right now. Just give him some time."
- Anxiety about what the future holds. For both you and the injured one. "I don't know what I'm going to do when the nurses are gone, I don't know if I can take care of him on my own."
- Anger at the person with a brain injury. "If he says 'I don't remember' one more time. I'm going to lose it. I'm going to snap." Or "That is the fourth time today she has asked me that question, I can't take this anymore."

- Becoming a turtle. Hiding in your shell will not make the world go away, nor will it make things any better. You may no longer want to stay in touch with your friends or do social activities that you did all the time. You may even say "I just don't care about anything anymore."

- Depression and hopelessness are common feelings at this time but if not looked after, you could be the one needing care. You may have feelings of not caring anymore, or feeling what's the use? Why should I keep trying? Depression will drag you down faster than anything; try not to fall into the trap of it. You do have a choice.

- Exhaustion, where you don't have the energy to do anything. Completing daily tasks and chores becomes an overwhelming experience because of your fatigue.

- Lack of sleep can cause many problems. You may wake up many times in the middle of the night, or have bad dreams or nightmares about the situation. Maybe your mind cannot stop racing and it feels like a television on which someone keeps changing the channel on you. Lack of sleep can be the cause of many problems.

- Emotional overload. I often say that people with acquired brain injury wear their emotions on their sleeves, but I now see that caregivers do also. You may cry when you hear a sad song or for no reason at all, you're often irritable. Simple little things that you would dismiss before, such as running out of dog food, now become a big emotional event and is the start of a fight. "You knew the dog food was low, why the hell didn't you pick up more?"

- Memory problems and lack of concentration sometimes go hand in hand and you will blame your lack of concentration on your bad memory. You may have trouble completing tasks that once seemed simple, or completing a regular task that you once did daily. "I used to read the newspaper daily, now I can't even focus on one story".

- Deteriorating health. You may be so focused on the person you're caring for, that you're denying yourself good health care, diet and exercise. You may find yourself losing or gaining weight. You may also develop other problems such as chronic headaches, back pain or high blood pressure and stress.

"All of life is chance. So take it! The person who goes furthest is the one who is willing to do and dare."
— Dale Carnegie, Author and Trainer

Reduce caregiver stress and overload

As a caregiver you need to take care of yourself in order to take care of your loved one. Just think of what would happen to your loved one if you are gone or become bedridden yourself. If you have ever travelled on an airplane, you will know that the first safety tip they show you if the cabin becomes depressurized is to put your oxygen mask on first before you help someone else. This makes perfect sense because you can't help other people with their breathing if you cannot breathe yourself.

"Take care of yourself first."

I really believe that the caregivers are the forgotten ones. Many people think only about the injured person, but I believe people should think more about the caregivers and ways to help reduce their stress. The caregiver is probably the most important person in a recovering person's life. Not only do they take care of the recovering person, but everything else falls on their shoulders. They have to take care of themselves and their children, the bills, the home and car maintenance, making meals and cleaning, the list goes on and on.

Caregivers should have a national holiday in their honor

because they are super people. Unfortunately in many cases, caregivers have to put up with a lot of hassles. I know my wife did and for a long time I wondered why she stayed with me. I would have left myself for the way I was acting. So on behalf of all people living with a brain injury, I would like to thank all of the caregivers and apologize to all of you who may have been emotionally hurt. My hope is that you can reduce a lot of your stress by reading these next few tips. Just try a few and I'm sure they'll work because you deserve to have a lot less stress in your life for everything you do.

Ways to reduce caregiver stress and overload

- Learn as much as you can about brain injury. As my friend Carol says, "Knowledge is power." There are many books and websites you can use for information. The more you understand the effects of brain injury, the easier it will be to identify with your loved one and what they may be going through. As a caregiver, you may find comfort in knowing that what you are experiencing is common. You are not unique in your anguish and its effects.

- Be realistic about the healing process and the amount of time it takes. Every injury is different. No two are the same so there is no straight answer as to when your loved one will recover. But know that it does take time, patience and love. It doesn't happen overnight, it happens over time.

- Get to know yourself and what you are capable of doing. You can't do everything on your own. So get your priorities in order, whatever they may be and write them down. For awhile you may have to give up something you love to do in order to make time for your loved one.

- Have a good belly laugh! Laugher is a natural stress reliever that helps to lower blood pressure, slows your heart rate and breathing rate and relaxes your muscles. There is nothing funny about a brain injury, but it is important to look on the lighter side of life. It is impossible to be sad or angry while you're laughing; if you don't believe me just try it. It is important to have a good laugh with the brain injured person because laughter releases endorphins into the brain which causes a sense of well-being and also reduces levels of pain and anxiety.

- Watch your diet and choose food carefully. You may not realize it but the food you are eating may be causing some of your stress. Inadequate nutrition increases stress on your body. Fatty foods full of sugar as well as processed foods seem to increase stress in most people. Lean meat, chicken, whole grains, fresh fruits and vegetables seem to decrease stress. You may think "Let's order a pizza, I'm too stressed to cook." Give it a second thought.

- Exercise can greatly reduce stress. Even if you take a ten minute walk around the hospital or down the street, it will help reduce your stress levels immensely. You will also find that you can think a little more clearly after a walk.

- Become better at breathing. While visiting someone in a hospital recently, I couldn't help but notice signs everywhere: "Breath deeply." I asked a nurse, "What's up with the signs?" She said "Stress can cause shallow breathing" which means that your body won't get enough oxygen to fully relax. Learn to breathe more slowly and deeply from your abdomen. One way to do this is to imagine that you have a small beach ball behind your belly button, which you slowly inflate and deflate. Practice that for awhile and you'll notice a great reduction in stress.

- Squish the ANTS (automatic negative thoughts). Most of our anxiety is self-induced, meaning that we reap what we sow. If you often think the worst case scenarios are going to happen, they usually do. Start thinking about the good things in life and how well things are going to be in the future. You will see that good things do come your way. Think positive. Read positive books or listen to some good music that will cheer you up. Squish those damn ANTS!

- Get used to your feelings being on an up and down roller coaster. Accept that you will have feelings of being happy, angry, guilty, embarrassed and sad, and know that there is no right or wrong way to feel at this time. Let your feelings out, it's okay to cry. You may want to pound on the pillow or go outside and scream in the car. Whatever it is, don't be shy. Let your feelings out and don't let them bottle up.

- Join a support group. There are many people out there going through the same thing you are. You are not alone. Ask your nurse or health care provider for a list of support groups in your area. It can really help to reduce your stress if you can talk to someone going through the same thing as you are. Chances are you will also receive many helpful tips that can help in so many ways on your journey of recovery. It is also nice to know that you have the support of people with similar experiences, that are willing to share their thoughts and feelings, and are also there to listen.

Develop a calming ritual to help you unwind at the end of the day. Do things that bring inner peace, such as reading, listening to music or meditating.

Therapy

Here are some different types of therapy that may help you in your recovery.

Speech and Communication

Having difficulty speaking and communicating may be the most frustrating part of your entire recovery, because if people do not understand what you are saying, or trying to say, it will make everyone's life very difficult. It can be very frustrating trying to get a message across without a brain injury, and with one, the frustration is compounded.

With that said, I also believe that speech and communication therapy is the most rewarding. Once you have reached your goals, it is an amazing feeling when you can clearly express what you are thinking.

Many of the people that I have met over the years have very similar speech and communication difficulties. The following are just a few of the most common difficulties and examples.

I have trouble finding words

You know what you want to say but the words just won't come out. For example you want to say, "I put it in the stove" and what comes out of your mouth is "The one thing, they are there that that thing!" which does not make any sense as you are pointing to the stove like a small child, frustrated with not finding the right words. You know what you want to say, but for some reason, the words stick to the tip of your tongue and will not come out. The harder you try, the more frustrated you become.

- Tips for survivor: slow down, you know what you want to say, think for a minute and ask yourself, "What does this thing do"? For example you could say, "That thing you cook on" or "That thing that heats food." When the front door is locked, climb the side window to find the word you're looking for or find another way to describe it, and the word will come to you. I found it very helpful to close my eyes and visualize the words I wanted to say, and then repeat them in my head over and over again.
- Tips for the caregiver: don't finish the patient's words or sentences, but do help them find the words by asking questions and creating thoughts. This way you can cue them to find the right word. For example, you could ask the person "What thing? Over there? What

does it do? Does it heat your food?" This way you'll know exactly what the person is talking about. The stove and not the fridge. I found cueing is a very helpful strategy in word finding.

What the @#%$ did he just say?

People with a brain injury will say things that are inappropriate. I often found myself apologizing after being sharply reminded that what I had said was inappropriate. Things would come out of my mouth that you would never hear me say in a million years before the injury. We are all human and we all have thoughts, many of which we would normally keep to ourselves. The only way I can describe it is that your brain is like a coffee filter and with a brain injury that coffee filter is torn, and sometimes it allows the grinds to get out.

For example, you take your wife out to a restaurant and you see a person who has done you wrong and you think "He's a jerk" and that thought stays in your mind. But with a brain injury that thought goes right from your brain to your tongue and you blurt out, "You're a jerk" right in the restaurant and embarrass yourself and your wife. (I am not being sexist here. I have met many women with brain injuries who have done the exact same thing. It's not just men.)

- Tips for the survivor: before anything comes out of your mouth, make sure that is what you want to say. In the beginning this is very difficult because your coffee filter is torn and only you have the power to fix it. The way to repair this torn filter takes time and practice, so before you speak, count to five or ten and make sure that's what you want to say. If you can practice this a little every day you can keep the thoughts in your head that should stay in your head.
- Tips for the caregiver: expect this to happen. If you are aware that at some point this is going to happen, you will not fly off the handle when it does occur and

you can deal with it in a calm and respectful manner. Let them know they should keep those thoughts to themselves and perhaps think next time before they speak. Don't kid yourself by thinking it won't happen. "My wife would never say that. She is respectable woman." Like I said earlier, we are all human.

I can't cope with noisy environments

With a brain injury it may be difficult to follow a conversation in a noisy environment such as a shopping mall or restaurant. I found it very difficult to be in a large crowd when many people were having different conversations. You can overcome this problem by working on a few strategies right in your own home. Start by having a conversation with a family member, and make sure all of the background noises are turned off, such as the radio and TV. Just talk back and forth, and then review what was said to make sure you were clear and there are no misunderstandings.

I found it very helpful to do this every day and little by little I was getting better. Eventually when you realize your concentration is getting better, you can introduce some background noise such as turning the radio on low and practicing again and again to make sure what is being said is also being understood. That should help prepare you for following a conversation in a noisy environment.

"Find the good. It's all around you. Find it, showcase it and you'll start to believe it."
— Jesse Owens, Olympic Gold Medal Athlete

CNN Therapy

This is one that I'm very proud of, not because it works so well for me, but because I discovered it with my speech therapist one day during a session. You see when people get hungry enough they will eat almost anything. I was hungry for knowledge, wanting to know how I could get better faster.

My speech therapist was amazing and very helpful. Because of economics, I was only seeing her three days a week for about an hour each time. She showed me so many strategies to overcome the difficulties I was struggling with. I had a craving to be better, so I had to think of another way that I could practice my speech and reading while Christine was gone.

It turns out it was right in front of me on the TV. You've got it! CNN. Who would've thought that I could overcome so many difficulties watching Anderson Cooper reporting all over the world? CNN had everything I needed to improve my speech, reading, memory and confidence and best of all it was free and available to me 24 hours a day.

Let me explain how it worked for me. Don't get me wrong, you will still get the best benefit from working with a speech language therapist. But if one isn't available where you live, or you don't have the funding, here are some things you can do.

This is not a plug for CNN. There are many channels out there and if you love sports, ESPN has the same type of format. The same goes for business CNBC or Breakfast Television for a fun morning show. Find what interests you and it will be much easier.

As you watch CNN you will notice a ticker-tape sliding across the bottom of the screen. What I would do is try to read each word as they passed by. In the beginning it was difficult to get one or two in a row but that didn't matter because I was alone and had all the time in the world. No one was there judging me or rushing me. In the beginning I would also turn the volume off. That was very helpful. The words will repeat again and again helping you with your memory. It seems very slow in the beginning.

I would say a few words like "Emirates airline profits

increase". After a few months I was able to read full sentences such as "President declares all troops will be coming home for Christmas". I was also able to remember them because it was repeated again and again all day long. It was also a boost to my confidence, because now I was able to start a conversation about current events and because I read and reread these stories, they stuck in my memory bank.

As my confidence grew, I graduated to the next step and turned up the volume on the TV. That simulated an environment where I was surrounded by people talking, while I was trying to read the ticker-tape. It was very frustrating in the beginning but in the end it was very helpful. It helped me to focus on what I was doing, rather than paying attention to the background noise.

Eventually I was able to read at the speed the words were passing by and this is a very natural rate of speech. One thing I would have to say to survivors is that you will have to participate in these activities every day and work at them.

You're not going to improve by just sitting around waiting for people to show up and help you. You have to take the initiative to help yourself. It does not matter what type of therapy it is or the obstacle you are trying to overcome. If you persist and truly work at your goal, you will find a way and it may not be the way someone shows you. Sometimes you will find your own way. As long as you are trying, you are moving towards long term improvement. Perseverance will always pay off. Perseverance really means doing the things you don't want to do, and doing them anyway.

"One way to keep momentum going is to have constantly greater goals."
— Michael Korda, Publisher

Occupational Therapy

This is a very important therapy to help get you back on

your feet. In the beginning I had no idea what it was about. My first therapist was Gary Warman, a nice guy who spoke very calmly to me. When he came to my house for the first time he brought a jar full of quarters, nickels and dimes. He poured the jar out onto my table and asked me to count a dollar-thirty-five. At that time it was the price of a cup of coffee. I was annoyed. How dare he come into my house and insult my intelligence?

As it turns out, I could not count money to pay for things, so Gary showed me some strategies to help me overcome some of my difficulties. But after the first day I told my wife I did not want to see him again. I felt very ashamed of my shortcomings. The next day Gary returned for another session and after he left my wife said, "I thought you didn't want to see him again?" I replied very sheepishly, "Well yesterday he found some things in me I didn't think I could do, I just want to see if he can find some more". And man did he ever!

I was amazed at the things I was capable of doing when someone put some faith in me and gave me some guidance.

Gary was also somehow able to ease the pain over time and my embarrassment faded as my confidence grew. He also helped me find myself again through ways I never thought of. He would say "There is always a way." Sometimes I would get frustrated with a task and get pissed off, saying "It can't be done." But he would show me a way.

I remember early on my goal was to make dinner, but because of my broken arm and very little feeling in my fingers, not to mention very little fine motor skills, it was not safe for me to cut the vegetables. Gary said, "There is a way!" We drilled a hole in my cutting board and put a meat thermometer through the bottom. I then pushed the potato though the metal spear. That held the vegetables in place and allowed me to safely cut them. To most people it may seem like no big deal, but for me it was huge and a big step towards independence. Every week I would learn something new or improve on something old. Looking back, Gary brought me a long way in a short time. Thank you, Gary.

After about two years, Gary was offered a job in another city that would be better for him and his family, so he moved. I have to tell you my heart blew a fuse when he gave me the news. Please let this be a bad dream! You have brought me so far and I still have a long way to go. "How am I going to do this?" I thought to myself.

Along came Claudia Maurice, my new Occupational therapist and at the same time I received a new case manager, Pat Saunoris. All I could think of was how hard I had worked to get where I was, and how I would have to start all over again because these new people wouldn't know what was going on in my life. Boy was I wrong!

These two women did a wonderful job understanding my needs and desires. All of a sudden it seemed like everything was happening so fast. I was enrolled back in high school and started driver training, which my first case manager did not think I was capable of doing.

The first thing Claudia did was help me to get organized. I was so caught up in the never ending trivial tasks that constantly come at you like email, TV and visitors, that I didn't realize how much of a negative impact disorganization had on my recovery. To me it just became a way of life and I accepted it.

Claudia showed me that I could be organized and productive with just a little planning each day. Every day we planned a list of tasks for me to accomplish. I probably had 20 or 30 things on the list but again Claudia shared with me that I was only setting myself up for disappointment with so many things on my list. We started again from scratch. In the beginning we agreed there would only be 2 to 3 things on my list for the day. It doesn't sound very hard and it isn't. Do you know what happened with those 2 to 3 things? They got done and this gave me a feeling of accomplishment. I finally felt that I was doing something great and working towards a better future. As my confidence grew I was able to take on bigger tasks and feel good about starting a project.

Other things we worked on included returning to the work force in a meaningful way. I enrolled in the necessary university courses to become a rehabilitation therapist and workplace safety advocate. I believe I will do very well in that line of work because of my experience over the years. There are very few rehabilitation therapists that can look a person in the eye and say, "I know what you're going through."

Chapter Thirty-Seven
Beware of Rehab Overload

This is a short story of what happened to me, and a warning that I hope will save you a lot of time, stress and upset feelings.

When I finally had my mind set that I was going to work on my rehab full-time and be the best that I could be, I was so focused that nothing would stand in my way. I felt like I could take on the world.

Right there was the beginning of a series of problems, starting with unrealistically high expectations in a short time period and then eventually burnout.

In the beginning, everything seemed fine. It was all laid out for me. If I did this, this and this, I would reach my goal and solve all of the problems that had been bothering me.

I was self-motivated, determined to give 110%, and believed that anything was possible if I worked hard enough. I still believe that axiom is true but once in a while you have to step back and look at things from a different angle.

Being positive is great, but being realistic will avoid burnout and failure. So stay positive but also have realistic goals that you can talk about with your rehab workers, family and friends.

When I finally decided to take 100% responsibility for my life and take control of my rehabilitation, just like the first principle in *The Success Principles* states, it was exciting as starting a new job. I was full of energy and excitement. Perhaps in some ways I was too anxious with only one focus in mind, getting better.

After a month or so I started to realize that my expectations were not realistic. My energy and excitement decreased as did my self-confidence. Along with disappointment came confusion. "Why am I not getting better? I work hard every day. Something is wrong, is it me?" I started to become frustrated and bored with my rehabilitation.

Chronic fatigue became one of my biggest problems. My poor sleeping patterns had me feeling like a zombie so I was unable to focus on my goals. Depression and anxiety also played a part. I kept thinking to myself, "What's the use? I'm trying every day but nothing is happening." A negative attitude became the flavor of the day.

In fact I was trying so hard that I pushed my family to the back burner. I found out later that was a big mistake. I wanted to improve so badly that I couldn't focus on anything else at the time. The doctors call that 'perseveration'. Everything in my life was pushed aside so I could get better, but what I didn't see was that I was indeed pushing my life aside when I should have kept my family right beside me through thick and thin.

I spoke to my doctor about this and he suggested I take a break for a few weeks from my rehabilitation. I did exactly that and boy what a difference it made. It was almost like stepping out of my own body and having a look around and I have to say I didn't like what I saw.

To explain this I use an example of a hot air balloon. Think back to a time when you were stuck in traffic and feeling frustrated. Now just imagine viewing that traffic from a hot air balloon. It is the same traffic yet it is no longer frustrating when you can see it from a distance. You also may see some new routes you can take to avoid this frustration in the future.

After that small break I was able to see what was important to me and that I had to keep everything in perspective. My family is number one. My rehabilitation would become number two. I decided to work on my rehabilitation during the day. In a sense, getting better was now my full time job. But like a job, leave your work at work. Don't bring it home for your family, especially if you have a bad day. When you are at home "be at home." I have met many divorced people because they focused too much on their work when they were at home, rather than their families.

Remember that the rehabilitation is about you and your goals. It is important to set goals that fit your needs and not those of someone else. Trying to do and be what others want you to do and be can cause you frustration and burnout.

So spend some time with your family and get clear on the big questions, such as why you are here, what do you want most in life, and what are your passions? Most nights I was too tired to even watch television, but I learned to spend time with my son by laying on the couch with him, even if I was sleeping.

Getting a hobby or spending time with friends and family is also a great way to relax. Have some fun every day and make sure that your rehabilitation doesn't have an overpowering influence on your self-esteem and self-confidence. Enjoy the journey, have some fun and try not to take yourself too seriously.

"It is not the straining for great things that is most effective; it is the doing of the little things, the common duties, a little better and better."
— Elizabeth Stuart Phelps, Writer

Chapter Thirty-Eight

Psychic Vampires and Time Bandits

When recovering from a brain injury or depression, it is easy to be held captive by the 'psychic vampires' and 'time bandits'. If someone steals your watch or television, the police will help with the arrest. With psychic vampires and time bandits, the only crime-fighting tool you have is your mind and you are the only one who can use it. It is purely a state of mind.

A 'psychic vampire' is someone who sucks the energy right out of you. You know, that person who drops by and when you see them, you think "Oh no, what do they want now?" You feel deflated. Or you answer the phone and they start talking about how bad everything is and you can't even get a word in. When the conversation is over you feel sick to your stomach.

You must avoid these people at all costs and if you cannot totally avoid them, just spend considerably less time with them. This alone will lower your stress level. You should keep your mind closed against all people who depress or discourage you and seek the company of friends and family who encourage and support your goals and dreams. Remember it is easy for people to give you advice but ultimately you have to think and act for yourself.

The 'time bandit' is someone comes around and thinks you have all the time in the world, so why shouldn't they help you waste it?

Very often the psychic vampires and time bandits are the same people who want to bore you with "Oh, poor me" stories. And if you get caught up in their trap, it will only become a contest to see which one of you is worse off. Don't fall into this trap. If you cannot speak for yourself, let your caregiver or family members know that you do not want this person around. They may have some strategies to help avoid these unwanted visits or phone calls.

A great lesson I learned from Jack Canfield was to make a list of all the people I interact with on a monthly basis. My list had about twenty names. Beside each name I put a positive mark (+) or a negative mark (-). This would clearly point out the people in my life who either lifted my spirits and were a positive influence, or dragged me down and left me feeling deflated. The next step was to completely stop spending time, or considerably less time with the negative people. Yes, there were family members on the negative list. I must share with you that after doing this exercise, my stress level has gone from an 8 or 9 to a 1 for several years now. This exercise is the greatest form of stress reduction I have ever tried.

Now of course I am not suggesting you abandon your family and acquaintances overnight. There are some ways to clear the air before it comes to that. I feel the best way is to have a heart talk. A heart talk can involve 2-10 people to be effective. Many of us have been in situations where emotional tension builds up so much that communication breaks down and people grow apart. People cannot listen until they have first been heard. They need to first get whatever's bothering them "off their chest" and a heart talk will allow them to do that without feeling guilty, judged or shamed.

A heart talk is a very structured communication process in which eight agreements are strictly adhered to. This will create a feeling of safety that will allow a deep level of communication to occur without fear, condemnation, unsolicited advice, interruption or being rushed. You will need one "heart" which can either be made by cutting a piece of paper or you can use anything in the shape of a heart. Start by asking people to sit in a circle or around the table and first introduce the basic agreements that include:

1. Only the person holding the heart can talk.
2. Pass the heart gently to the left after your turn.
3. You may choose to pass.
4. You can talk only about how you feel.
5. You can't judge or criticize what anyone else has said.
6. You keep the information confidential.
7. You don't leave the talk until it's declared complete.
8. Be considerate of how long you talk.

Once the agreements are stated, you can begin with the first person who would like to share what is currently going on in their life. This is not a time for judging or blaming, just to share what is going on in their lives and how they are feeling. This allows everyone to be heard in a nonjudgmental way. Many times this can clear up a lot of confusion and miscommunication that has been building up over time and allows people to let go of resentments and old issues that are no longer a concern. Your heart talk will be complete when there is nothing left to say from any of the participants.

I would recommend that you visit www.livelovelaugh.com and obtain a copy of the heart talk book which includes a bright red heart insert with the eight key agreements.

"Time is a non-renewable resource."
— Doug Shaw, Graphic Designer

Chapter Thirty-Nine

Control

The only thing you can control is yourself, the thoughts you think, the words you say and the actions you take...

I have heard many stories from survivors about how other people (parents, kids, spouses and co-workers) will try to control them, their feelings, thoughts, emotions, actions and behavior. News flash: that doesn't work! It is like pushing a car uphill with a rope. It won't accomplish anything.

Rather than trying to control a person (which can only create tension), try to make agreements with that person. I found this very helpful. It was my speech language therapist, Christine, who introduced me to this concept.

I don't know if she planned this or not, but she would say things to me like, "Before I come back here on Tuesday, can we agree that you will try to read these words I left for you?" I would agree. We did this on a mutually agreed upon basis and really all agreements you make are with yourself. She didn't have control over me. What can be controlled or managed is our agreement, and this is a very mature and respectful way of doing things. From then on Christine and I enjoyed a more open and trusting line of communication. It was easier to discuss more uncomfortable subjects and things I had been avoiding or hiding from. Now that I was accountable for things, I no longer felt like a puppet on a string. I had feelings of self-respect and self-responsibility. It was a real confidence booster. When you are treated with respect you want to give some back. It's like the old saying, "Givers get."

One person I met with an acquired brain injury told me that his father said he was a disappointment, failure, and a burden on the family and that he was lazy, just laying around most days. He told me that he couldn't wait to move out and get away from him. You see, his father treated him like a second-class citizen with no respect, trying to control his son, Since "givers get", his father was given the same in return, no respect. The son has since moved to another town. I sometimes wonder if they will ever work it out or if the father will die a lonely man without his son at his side.

This situation may have been quite different if they had made some agreements with each other.

Looking back, everyone on my team made agreements with me. My doctor said, "Let's agree that you will not use any tool that operates with gas or electricity" (This was due to all of the incidents I had with tools. I call them 'incidents' and not 'accidents' because they could have been prevented if I had slowed down and assessed the situation). Anyway, I agreed.

My psychologist said, "Let's make a deal. When you feel angry or anxious, go to that quiet place in your head and breathe slowly and relax." I agreed, and after working hard on those things for a few years, I have not been angry since. Disappointed yes but not angry.

One of my surgeons told me that if I agreed to follow the physiotherapy plan and didn't do anything strenuous for a long time, I might be able to keep my arm. "Gee thanks, Doc!" Well, four surgeries later over a period of two and a half years and wearing a cast on my arm for over two years, I was able to keep my arm. It's not very strong but it's there. I kept my agreements and they kept theirs.

These agreements can be made by brothers and sisters, wives and husbands and they really work. If you can put it on paper and sign it, it will make you more accountable because talk is cheap

Agreements can be big or small, but it is important to communicate what all parties agree on. Like most people I know, we all skipped the mind reading course in school. Let other people know what you are thinking. All people must be present to make the agreement so that everyone understands their responsibilities. No bullying, bossing or "It's my way or the highway" attitude. All parties must agree, that's why it's called an agreement. It must also be two-sided and not one-sided. You must work with your team. It takes good communication, especially at home where you spend most of your time. This is another opportunity to have a heart talk.

When the home team is working smoothly, home becomes a security blanket in a stressful world. And when it is not working smoothly, home can become a source of stress and a place you do not want to be.

You must talk with everyone openly, honestly and respectfully. And they should talk to you in the same way. If you don't talk about your problems, they will never get solved. With a lack of communication, molehills will turn into mountains and the longer the silence continues, the worse things get. This is why it is important to have a weekly household meeting just so everyone knows where they stand … who does what chores, who pays what bills, and so on.

These types of meetings can easily prevent an accumulation of problems that will bottle up and eventually blow up. With this in mind, start today and make your first agreement. You'll soon see the improvement this makes in your life.

"The past cannot be regained, although we can learn from it;
the future is not yet ours even though we must plan for it.
Time is now. We have only today."
— Charles Hummell, Writer

Chapter Forty

Changes

You may experience changes in behavior and personality but remember, the only thing you can really control is your own behavior. Stop trying to control the lives of your friends, neighbors, partners and families because this will drain your precious energy and leave you an unhappy person. You can't make anybody do anything.

Many of us believe that other people can be 'made' to behave the way we want them to. Common annoyances include not closing the fridge door, learning how to control anger, learning how to speak and communicate fluently. Some people use tactics such as guilt, shame, force or bribery to change another person's behavior.

These tactics may produce short-term results, but from my experience, it will only last as long as the pressure is on. For example: following your children around the house and making sure they shut off every light. When you stop correcting them, they will stop too.

You can't get people to change just because you want them to, or because you think life will be better if they follow your rules. They will only change if they are motivated to do so. We all do things in life for either reasons or feelings. Most behavior is motivated by a payoff of one kind or another. Perhaps you quit smoking because you're expecting your first grandchild and you would like to see him/her grow up and get married. That's a big motivator if I've ever seen one. It probably works better than constantly being nagged at about the cost of cigarettes or your stinky clothes.

The same holds true for rehabilitation. You must look at the positive results that will occur when you work hard on your recovery.

For example, I had lunch this week with a friend that also has an acquired brain injury. He had decided to take the summer off from his speech therapy. When I asked him when he was going to resume it, he had considered not going back because he hasn't seen much improvement. I shared with him the idea that you cannot sit at home and hope to improve your speech. You must participate every day and you will see very little improvement unless you work hard at your recovery.

Hope alone will not provide results. Period. You must have a plan and stick to it. I understand if you want to take a break from some of the therapies once in awhile. It's a healthy idea to step back and look at the progress you've made and the direction that you're going. There were many days I felt that I did not want to do anything but it is also important to get back on track and continue your recovery until you are satisfied, and give up for nothing less.

Dr. Davidson often said to me, "A professional hockey player practices every day for hours and hours. He knows how to skate backwards and how to shoot a puck. Yet they still go out day after day and practice. That's what you must do if you want to be at the top of your game. Whether it is your speech, controlling your anger, or learning to drive again, you must have the desire to participate every day."

I know this because I stuck with speech therapy for over five years. Was it all fun and games? Not really, especially in the beginning. It was long, frustrating, boring and made me very tired. I would look at something simple and know what it is, point at it, have the word on the tip of my tongue, but it would not come out. Pointing like a small child and saying, "That, that, that." Yet still, a simple word would not come out. That's frustration and that's what makes a lot of people give up on themselves. "I can't get it, so why even try?" were the thoughts that went through my head. Many, many times. I now have so much compassion for people all over the world who have moved to different countries and don't know the language. I now know what it feels like to talk and have no one understand me and the frustration have, knowing exactly what they want to say yet they can't easily communicate.

So often I wanted to give up. And this was only because of the emotional pain I was causing myself through my perceived failure. It was a very emotional roller coaster, not being able to read or say the words I was looking at and not being able to remember the ones that I could read and say. To me, recovery was a long journey that had no end in sight. I just could not imagine being able to read and speak at a level where I would feel comfortable again.

I was very lucky to have my speech therapist, Christine, who believed in me when I didn't believe in myself. I have since seen her work wonders with other people. A friend of mine was in a bad snowmobile accident that left him in a coma for months and also with an acquired brain injury. I went to see his family in the hospital and explained some of the things they might experience when he would wake up and all of the wonderful things that would follow. When he came out of the coma he had no speech ability. I recommended my speech therapist, Macpherson Communication, to his family. He eventually retained their services and this made a big difference in his recovery.

It has now been several years since the accident and his speech has improved tremendously. After a long recovery, he has returned to work and continues to practice his rehabilitation exercises every day.

The same thing applies to your recovery. You may not see the small changes every day, but if you work daily towards very small improvements, you will eventually see massive improvements over time. I made a commitment to myself to change daily in the smallest amount possible, one percent. I would try every day to improve just one percent a day. It may have been learning a new word or becoming a better father but by improving one percent a day I was able to do a complete transformation in one year and that was a huge turnaround.

I continue to try and change one percent a day, to this day. Change by the yard is hard, by the inch is a cinch!

"There are no secrets to success. It is the result of preparation, hard work and learning from failures."
— Colin Powell, American Secretary of State

Chapter Forty-One
Is Now a Good Time to Have an Anxiety Attack?

Depending on its severity, anxiety causes feelings that range from mild nervousness to doom and gloom or panic.

What's going on?
Anxiety is our biological alarm. When we perceive danger we respond by becoming anxious. A certain amount of anxiety is normal and even productive.

For example, if a parent has children playing in the swimming pool and the children have become suddenly quiet, the parent may rush to investigate and possibly prevent an accident as a result of the parent's anxiety. We respond to anxiety emotionally with a complex range of feelings including fear, dread and anger which causes physical responses such as tense muscles, racing hearts, shallow breathing and sweaty palms and feet. It will also raise the acidic levels in your body.

I have kept in contact with a teacher from high school and he has been a chronic worrier since I was a kid. His chronic worrying and anxiety has caused many health problems including tooth decay, stomach problems and now a mental breakdown that has forced him to move from his home to an assisted living facility. Out of all the people I have met, he should be the last one to worry, yet it is sending him to an early grave as he continually obsesses over problems that do not exist. I spoke with his brother while visiting him one day at the nursing home and his brother shared with me that he has been a worrier since childhood.

Intellectually, anxiety often interferes with clear thinking. Behaviorally, we exhibit the "fight or flight" response, preparing ourselves for self-defense or escape. In the early days this response was useful to the individual because when you were in danger, it would give you a boost of energy to get away from whatever was putting you in danger, like running away from a bear. Unfortunately, the anxiety alarm sometimes goes awry and we confuse safe situations as dangerous or mildly threatening situations as life-threatening. Many scientists now believe our anxiety alarm system is influenced by a complex interaction of genetics, illnesses, drugs and our history of traumatic events such as a car accident, stroke, assault or being at war.

Panic attacks or anxiety attacks can happen anywhere. There is no right time to have one. But they can be prevented.

I remember being in a car and getting short of breath, thinking the worst and grabbing the dash saying, "Slow down!" or "Oh no, we're going to crash!" Or being in a grocery store and suddenly feeling dizzy and short of breath as if an elephant was standing on my chest. On that occasion I told my wife we had to go. I left the shopping cart in the aisle and ran to the truck where I began to cry. "What the hell is going on in my head?" I thought to myself.

I was hospitalized several times for anxiety attacks and each time I was rushed right into the emergency room because these symptoms were the same as a heart attack. When you arrive at a hospital with these symptoms, you take priority. The attacks increased in intensity and frequency to the point that I did not want to go out in public. I started living like a hermit. I would stay home and only see people when they came to my house. Even the therapists came to my house instead of me going to their office. It was almost as if my home was a security blanket.

I would jump out of my skin if the door slammed or a dog barked. I'm sad to admit that we got rid of our family dog for this reason. When hurricane Katrina hit, I felt as if I were right there in the TV. I started crying and had a feeling of doom and gloom.

I now know these are common experiences that happen after a brain injury. Luckily, there is help and I reached out for that help. "I want to be better", I thought. All of this negative thinking was making me sick. Dr. Davidson reached down and helped me out of this huge emotional hole that I had dug for myself. By showing me how to relax and look at things differently I was able to change my way of thinking.

Relaxation was the key to unlocking the door that was holding me back. I owe him a debt that can never be repaid, other than to share some strategies on how to overcome anxiety and depression.

I was already on enough pills to choke a horse and I didn't want to take any more for anxiety, so I said I would try anything to make this stop. The relaxation techniques worked really well. It didn't happen overnight but after a few months I started to feel much better and was able to control the attacks with simple thoughts. Ninety-nine per cent of the bad things I had thought about never happened and the one per cent that did were not nearly as bad as I had pictured.

This is also the time I started applying, "Become an inverse paranoid" from *The Success Principles*. Instead of thinking the worst and believing the world was out to get me, I began to think the world was out to help me in every aspect of my life. I began asking myself, "What is the opportunity in this situation?"

Anxiety is very uncomfortable, so anxious people will absolutely try to avoid situations that make them feel more uncomfortable. I discovered that this avoidance can have a very serious negative impact on one's life.

One day I was getting coffee and a fellow in the coffee shop shouted at me, "Hey, how have you been? I haven't seen you for a few years. I heard you went a little crazy for awhile from that accident!" I could feel my face turning red. I was angry and embarrassed at the same time. It took everything I had to not walk over and throw my coffee in his face. "Relax, Forrest!" I told myself. I just nodded and smiled. Because of my fear of confrontation, I was overly nice to people who were not nice to me.

Looking back I can see where that guy was coming from. In his eyes I was acting odd, running out of stores crying, avoiding people like the plague, and being alone in my house because I didn't want to socialize with people. I can certainly see how that would seem odd to someone. I have since forgiven him for his lack of understanding about what goes on while someone is struggling with depression and brain injury. Later on we had coffee while I explained some things I had gone through.

That day I helped him understand and I helped myself understand that there needs to be more information available to the public on brain injuries. I know Brian is a decent guy who means well; he was trying to use his sense of humor to break the ice that day.

I hope you can take something from this story and realize that people are not mind readers. Try to look at things through the other person's viewpoint, like Brian's for example. What would make him say those things? We should educate people on brain injury and depression so that we can all live a good life. Avoidance is not the answer, it is the problem. It only makes things worse. Consider that all over the world, people are sleeping on the streets and living in cardboard boxes. They have a million more reasons to believe they've run out of options than you do. If you are reading this book in a warm comfortable place right now you are richer than ninety percent of the people on the planet. So stand your ground and state your case. After the first time you explain your situation to someone, it gets easier to do and your anxiety will fade.

If you struggle with anxiety, most schools and workplaces will accommodate your needs when you explain your situation. Schools will allow you to take tests and examinations in a quiet room without distractions. Many workplaces may find a different position for you or a quiet place to work, but only if your situation is explained to them. They are not mind readers so let people know what is going on as soon as you can. In no way should you use your emotional struggles as a crutch or to take advantage of people's kindness. Just make them aware of what is going on and things can run a lot smoother and you will have less anxiety.

You may require a note from your doctor, which should not be a problem. Your doctor should be happy if you decide to return to work or school. My doctor was. His only advice was, "Don't beat yourself up and know that you are going to make mistakes and learn from them" and I sure did.

Chapter Forty-Two
Rental versus Ownership

After my accident I felt like a renter in my own body. What I mean it is that my body was a place to live, but I didn't really care about it like an owner would. A person who rents a home or apartment may not care if the lawn gets cut this week or if the dog runs inside with dirty paws or maybe even if wine is spilled on the carpet. Look at people's attitude towards a rental car versus a car they own. They may think, "It's not mine so why should I care?"

When you have ownership of a home, you take pride in it. You cut the lawn, wash the windows and vacuum so that when you have friends or family visiting, you can be proud of what you own. As a renter in my own body, I didn't take care of myself the way I should have by eating right, taking care of my appearance, staying physically active. I just kept thinking that I would wake up in my old body with the old me in the mirror. Well I can say stop waiting for that day. You have to work for it and work hard for your recovery. It's not just going to appear. If you want to chop down a tree it doesn't matter how big it is. By taking 5 swings a day with an axe, eventually it will fall down. The same principle holds true for your goals. Just work at it every day and eventually you will be where you want to be. You will own your future.

I follow the rule of five every day and it has made a huge impact on my life. Everyday I write down five things I will do in that day towards my goal and it has paid off more than I can be grateful for.

"To swear off making mistakes is very easy. All you have to do is swear off having ideas."
— Leo Burnet, Advertising Pioneer

Chapter Forty-Three

Buy Now, Pay Later

This expression has become a way of life for many people. You can enjoy the new car now without paying or working for it for many months. With brain injury the opposite is true. You must first deal with the unpleasant and frustrating parts of recovery before you can celebrate the victory phase of life.

"You can't learn to swim without getting in the pool".
— Jack Canfield, Bestselling Author and Coach

Delayed rewards means you must work on your problems now, no matter how frustrating they are, in order to enjoy a good life in the future. Being serious about your recovery must become a habit. A habit is a cable in which each day we weave a thread until eventually it cannot be broken. This also holds true for bad habits, so be careful. I fell into this trap myself. I would lie around on the couch until noon, then maybe make something to eat, wait for the therapists to show up and then take a rest. This went on for a long time and became a bad habit. I just simply became lazy and allowed this to happen. Fortunately I was able to snap out of it, but it wasn't easy. I started exercising a little every day and that helped me regain my energy. There are no quick fixes for many things in life. Everything takes time, whether it's working on your anger or anxiety or getting out of a rut of laziness. They all take time but if you put your mind to it, you can do anything.

Remember if you have the power to build a habit, you have the power to break it also.

"Only those who will risk going too far can possibly find out how far one can go."
— T.S. Eliot; Poet, Critic, and Editor

Chapter Forty-Four
Sex, Drugs and Rock and Roll

This story sounds like something you would hear from a rock star but it's a funny and personal little story that happened to me.

Sex was different after acquiring a brain injury. For the longest time I had very little desire for sex, probably because of my depression and constant pain. It was a very weird time in my life. I was taking many drugs for depression, and heavy doses of painkillers to manage the pain from surgeries on my face, arm and hips. I had the habit of taking the painkillers even if I was not in pain because they gave me a feeling that everything was fine. I could not see that the drugs were chemically disconnecting the fire alarm to my brain that would tell me if I was doing right or wrong.

I was also taking Arecept to improve my memory, sleeping pills and many other pills that I don't remember. All of the drug side effects must have counteracted each other. It got to the point where I thought my sex drive was bi-polar. "I want to have sex." "No I don't." When I was in the mood for sex I had to make an appointment so that the Viagra would kick in. It was so embarrassing going to the drugstore to ask for Viagra in my early 30's that I would ask my brother to drive me to the next town where I would fill my prescription.

This was also a very frustrating time in my life and I compounded my problems by changing the amount of medication I would take without consulting my doctor. One time I quit taking all of my pills because I thought it was ridiculous having to use Viagra because of the other drug side effects. "Note to self. Not a good idea!" You see when I quit taking all of my pills for pain and depression I immediately became a miserable person, angry and upset at the world. Who wants to have sex with a person like that? Damned if you do and damned if you don't.

Eventually over the years I have been able to wean myself off all the medication under strict doctor's supervision. Before even considering the idea of changing your medication, please consult your doctor. I was able to do this through an exchange program. Yes, an exchange program.

Over a period of one year I traded my medication for a pair of running shoes and an iPod. I used to say that I was too stressed to exercise, but little did I know that exercise was one of the best stress reducers ever.

The other thing that lifted my mood was rock & roll music. It's amazing just how quickly your mood can change when you listen to some upbeat fast-paced music or whatever makes you smile. The exercise combined with music gave me a whole new outlook on things, and I soon began to see the positive changes I had made.

You can also make these positive changes. Decide today to get up off the couch and go for a walk and just see how good you feel.

I would like to repeat again.

Never stop taking your medication without first consulting your doctor.

For a long time I thought there was no way to get off the pills because I needed them to get through the day. I can share with you that I have been off all medication since August 2007 and the world is much brighter and clearer and so full of opportunity. While on the pills I could not see the horizon. For anyone who decides to make the change I congratulate you. It is not easy yet it is well worth it.

"When I examine myself and my methods of thought, I come to the conclusion that the gift of fantasy has meant more to me than my talent for absorbing positive knowledge."
— Albert Einstein, Physicist

Chapter Forty-Five

Coat of Many Colors

"Coat of many colors" is a song by Dolly Parton that I first heard as a child. I was only about eight years old but that song has stuck in my head my entire life because I could relate to it so well growing up. As a kid, I wore second hand and hand-me-down clothes and remember other kids at school laughing at me when I wore pants that went well above my ankles.

I think everyone wears a coat of many colors and that one is poor only if they choose to be. That being said, the same still applies today in our journey. We all wear a coat of many colors. The one we are born with is full of energy and excitement, love and wonder, imagination and dreams. Sadly after a traumatic event, so many of us seem to sew on new dark patches of fear and anxiety, stress, doubt and disbelief in oneself. Eventually your coat is covered with these new grey and black patches and we become comfortable in our new coats of fear and doubt and we start seeing things in grey and black, believing that there is no hope, so why even try.

Negativity fertilizes the weeds of depression. The more patches you sew on the coat, the heavier it will become and before long, the coat becomes so heavy it drags you down.

Someone can only be a victim if they choose to be one. Today would be a good day to take that coat off and start new, by shaking off those dirty patches and begin to see those bright colors again. Just look around you. There are so many people who are willing to help. All you have to do is ask and you'll be amazed how good it feels to have a sense of self-respect, well-being and happiness. It is that simple. I didn't say easy, I said simple. Nothing worth doing is ever easy, but it can be simple.

Chapter Forty-Six
Acres of Diamonds

The Acres of Diamonds has been told by Russell Conwell, over 5,000 times in his speeches. It is about an African farmer who heard tales about other farmers who had made millions by discovering diamond mines. These tales so excited the farmer that he could hardly wait to sell his farm and go prospecting for diamonds himself. He sold the farm and spent the rest of his life wandering the African continent searching unsuccessfully for the gleaming gems that brought such high prices on the markets of the world. Finally, worn out and in a fit of despondency, he threw himself into a river and drowned.

Meanwhile, the man who had bought his farm happened to be crossing the small stream on the property one day, when suddenly there was a bright flash of blue and red light from the stream bottom. He bent down and picked up a stone. It was a good-sized stone, and admiring it, he brought it home and put it on his fireplace mantel as an interesting curiosity.

Several weeks later a visitor picked up the stone, looked closely at it, hefted it in his hand, and nearly fainted. He asked the farmer if he knew what he'd found. When the farmer said, no, that he thought it was a piece of crystal, the visitor told him he had found one of the largest diamonds ever discovered. The farmer had trouble believing that. He told the man that his creek was full of such stones, not all as large as the one on the mantel, but sprinkled generously throughout the creek bottom.

That farm turned out to be one of the most productive diamond mines on the entire African continent. The first farmer had owned, free and clear … acres of diamonds. But he had sold them for practically nothing, in order to look for them elsewhere. The moral is clear: If the first farmer had only taken the time to study and prepare himself to learn what diamonds looked like in their rough state, and to thoroughly explore the property he had before looking elsewhere, all of his wildest dreams would have come true.

The thing about this story that has so profoundly affected millions of people is the idea that each of us is, at this very moment, standing in the middle of our own acres of diamonds. If we had only had the wisdom and patience to intelligently and effectively explore the work in which we're now engaged, to explore ourselves, we would most likely find the riches we seek, whether they be financial or intangible or both.

Before you go running off to what you think are greener pastures, make sure that your own is not just as green or perhaps even greener.

It has been said that if the other guy's pasture appears to be greener than ours, it's quite possible that it's getting better care. Besides, while you're looking at other pastures, other people are looking at yours.

Don't start looking elsewhere for your happiness. You know where it is.

Everything you need in life is within your reach.

Try a few of these ideas and see how you feel:

- Find someone who needs a hug
- Hand-write some thank-you letters
- Give time to a needy person
- Volunteer in your community
- Call up an old friend
- Open some doors and smile
- Go for a walk with your family.

"Generosity is giving more than you can, and pride is taking less than you need."
— Kahil Gibran, Poet and Novelist

Chapter Forty-Seven
Drummond Peet

Prince of the Forrest

I first met Drummond Peet in 2008 and he has become one of my closest friends and a great life mentor. I moved to my current house in 2006 and would often see Drum on his daily walk up my road with his trusty dog Duffy. I knew Drum was a local retired lawyer from town and very well respected in the community so I did not bother walking out to the road to introduce myself. I often wanted to connect with him but I thought, "Why would a busy lawyer like him want to stop and talk to me?" Little did I know he thought the same about me.

He told me later that he had heard a lot about me through the business community and someone told him I was a nice guy! But he did not want to bother me as he heard I was a very busy person and why would a young business man want to hang around a retired guy like him?

At this time Drum was unaware that I was recovering from a brain injury and had sold my businesses.

One day a neighbor from an adjoining farm introduced us and we have been great friends since then. I just wish we had met years prior to that date. I have learned so many great life lessons from Drum, like always trying to see things from the other person's viewpoint and also to give everyone twenty minutes. Don't judge a person in the first two minutes of meeting them because there is always two sides of every person, just as there are two sides to every story, and many other lessons that have helped make me the person I am today.

Our story reminds me of the childhood movie 'Bambi.' There is little Bambi looking across the forest floor at this large buck, the Prince of the forest, and Bambi says "Wow, look at that large deer with the big antlers, if only I could meet him he could teach me how to survive and fend for myself and escape from the hunters, but why would a big deer like that want anything to do with a little fawn like me?" As the large deer looks back from the top of the hill he says "Look at that young fawn, if only I could meet him, he could show me how to play and have fun again! We would have so much fun, I would love the chance to feel young again but why would a young fawn want anything to do with an old buck like me?" Does that sound familiar? So if you want to get to know a person, approach them and introduce yourself. You could be amazed at what lies ahead.

And just as the movie plays through, the larger, wiser deer (Drummond) is the Prince of this Forrest.

Remember, a stranger is a friend you have not met yet. Good luck on your journey!

"The art of living lies less in eliminating our troubles than
growing with them."
— Bernard Baruch, Government Adviser

Chapter Forty-Eight
12 Hugs to Happiness

I did not realize that giving and receiving 12 hugs per day would change my life so much. In February 2012, I met Jack Canfield in person for the first time. When I arrived at his training course in California, he gave me the biggest hug. It was only about an hour into the first day when Jack shared the advantages of hugs.

Jack shared a story of Virginia Satir, a well-known American author and social worker. Virginia stated that people need four hugs per day for survival, eight hugs a day for maintenance and 12 hugs a day for growth. Jack then went on to show an example of how to give a proper hug. Left ear to ear, heart to heart and that if you hug for at least 20 seconds it begins to release the bonding hormone and neurotransmitter oxytocin, which is a natural antidepressant.

Then things got interesting. Jack said "Now what I want you to do is stand up and mingle around the room and get some hugs from people", I have to say this was so far out of my comfort zone I wanted to run to the nearest fire escape.

You see growing up I don't ever remember being hugged. At a young age I developed the self belief that the people who are supposed to love you and take care of you (your parents) either leave you or hurt you. So I had developed an invisible shield around myself for my whole life and didn't allow anyone into my heart, that way I would not get hurt again.

For some reason that day in February I let my guard down and allowed myself to feel unconditional love for the first time in my life. The emotions I was feeling were very overwhelming in a good way. It was hard for me to believe that this is what it feels like to be loved. I also realized that day that I had never felt loved until I loved myself. It is very hard to describe the feelings I went through that day other than pure joy.

At the end of that day I ran up to my hotel room and explained to my wife what had happened and how much joy I was experiencing. I also shared with her that I had not let anyone in my heart including her up and to that point for the fear of being hurt. That day was also a turning point in my marriage, from that day on I was able to love and be loved, and that is something you cannot buy nor take away. From that day forward I committed to receiving and giving these 12 hugs per day.

I share this exercise in my workshops and keynote speeches and the comments I receive from people is that this is their favorite part. I also enjoy going to schools and old-age homes and sharing the hug process. It is sad but true that there are many people who have not had a hug in years.

During my keynote speech at the Global Leadership Summit in Jaipur, India, I shared the story of hugging and invited the crowd to stand up and get some hugs. When my speech was over a man in the audience stood up and shared an emotional story that his wife had passed away and today was the first time he had received a hug in 11 years. There was not a dry eye in the room and his story made me realize even more that we underestimate the power of the hug.

We are given many hugs as babies and as we grow older, they become less and less. My hope is to change that and see that as we grow older we will receive more and more hugs. My call to action for you is to go out today and start with four hugs, and then slowly increase the amount over time. I guarantee it will make a huge difference in your mental health and overall well-being.

We are all so busy with our hands and our eyes on our keyboards and cell phones, so ask yourself what is your heart and mind busy with? It is usually nothing important so go out and stretch your arms and give a hug!

Chapter Forty-Nine

Memory

I Almost Forgot!

I can't believe I am finished the book and I forgot to write a part about memory, well actually I do believe it.

I will keep this section short, just like my memory. It has been over a decade since my injury and I still have trouble with short-term memory. Fortunately, I have learned some strategies to overcome this little problem. First of all, admit it. That will make things so much better.

I often ask people to call and remind me of an appointment we have. Post-it-notes are one of my best friends because I write reminders for myself throughout the house. I will move them from one side of the mirror to the other because they somehow become invisible if they stay in one spot.

Another thing that helped me a lot in the beginning were flash cards. Don't feel embarrassed. Anything that helps is a good thing. I keep an erasable white board in my shower so I will not lose any thoughts that come to me. Day timers are also good, and today most people have them on a phone but I still prefer a good old-fashioned pen and paper over an electronic device. A piece of paper in front of me is still my best reminder.

My long-term memory is great. I still remember being in grade seven and wanted to go to the fall fair but I didn't have two pennies to rub together. I was at my friend Jeff's house said how much fun it would be to go to the fair with all the other kids. Jeff's mother went into her change jar and gave me a roll of dimes, five bucks, "Wow." I walked around that fair like a millionaire. It is a memory I will never forget. She was not rich, but she had a rich heart and she taught me a lesson that I try to pass on to other people.

If you can give of yourself, you will never be poor, and if currency was counted in friends and love, I would be the richest man alive.

Baseballs Don't Bounce

About the Author

 Forrest Willett is a #1
bestselling author
and mental health
consultant who speaks
around the world with
individuals and corporations.

Through his keynote speeches and workshops, Forrest promotes mental wellness, helping to decrease days off and sick leave, and to eliminate stigma in the workplace around meantl health.

Forrest is also a certified Success Principles trainer and his inspirational story is featured in the New York Times Bestseller The Success Principles by Jack Canfield with over one million books in print.

If you'd like to book Forrest to speak, you can connect with him in several ways:

- Website: http://www.forrestwillett.com/
- Facebook:https://www.facebook.com/profile.php?id=100007210304896
- YouTube: Forrest Willett

Can You Help?

If you liked this book and it was helpful to you, could you PLEASE leave a review on Amazon? Simply visit Amazon to leave your honest feedback on the book page!

Reviews are really important to the success of a book—so if you like (or don't like!) what you've read, PLEASE take 2 minutes to leave your honest review —I really appreciate it.

Testimonials

I have asked my wife, a friend, and some of the professionals that provided me with so much help over the years, to share with you their own thoughts of how they saw me through their eyes and the progress that I have made.

Julie Willett
My wife

October 6, 2002—this was the day that our lives changed in a matter of seconds.

It was a beautiful fall day. We were in the middle of renovating our home. My husband was busy working on our garage. We had a few workers and friends over working on our house.

I remember taking my friend and my son who was 2 years old at the time shopping for the day. Once we returned, I decided that I would go into the house and make dinner for everyone that was there helping out. During this time, my husband went on a test drive with someone who was interested in buying our car.

At approximately 6pm, one of my friends had come into the house and said that they had heard quite a few sirens going down the road. At this time I did not pay attention to the sirens.

Not too long after this, one of our friends who was on the fire department said there was an accident up the road and he would have to leave as he was on call. It was one of those moments, when you have that sick feeling. I thought, wow, my husband has been gone for quite a while and he should have been home by now. I didn't know why, I just knew I had to go. I asked my neighbor to watch our son and I said I would be right back.

Once I arrived at the scene, the road was completely closed off. I went as far as I could. Like I said before we had friends that were on the fire department. As Forrest was on this fire department as a volunteer for many years, I went over to one of our friends and asked him about the accident.

He just stared at me with tears in his eyes and didn't say a word. It was at that moment that I knew it was my husband who was in the accident. I was told that I couldn't go any closer. My whole body started to shake and go numb as my world stopped in time. A few minutes later a police officer came over and told me that there was a terrible accident. He wouldn't tell me any details, just that they were going to transport my husband to the hospital once they were able to extricate him from the wreckage.

When I arrived at the hospital, I was told the car my husband was in had left the road and went airborne into a field, flipping end to end. There was a passerby that had seen the whole thing happen, and if it wasn't for that person, **the police** wouldn't have located the car, as the road was not a busy one and the field they landed in was not visible from the road. My husband had been the passenger in the car. I still couldn't understand how the whole scenario had happened or why, I just knew that my husband was now in the hospital with multiple injuries and head trauma.

When I first saw my husband in the hospital, I couldn't believe it was him. I didn't recognize Forrest because his face was swollen and full of blood, he was missing teeth, and there were tubes and wires all over him. The thought of him this way still haunts me.

What followed would be many years of rehabilitation. Our lives turned upside down in a matter of seconds. The beginning was the hardest part. We were bombarded with people. Doctors, therapists, rehabilitation workers, social workers, everyone came to us at once. My husband had to learn to walk without falling, speak fluently, read, write and do everyday routines again like showering, getting dressed and brushing his hair. We also had a successful business that we couldn't just let go. I now had to run our business without his help.

I had to raise our son and help my husband get through his day. It was extremely stressful. Could I have just said "This isn't for me" and walked away? Sure, I suppose I could have. But I didn't. I loved my husband and my family too much. This was something we were going to do together.

And we did.

It is hard to believe the amazing transformation since the accident. Because of the accident, we have realized that Forrest was given another chance. Forrest now dedicates his time to helping other people who are struggling with brain injuries and mental health issues.

I am so proud of my husband and all of his accomplishments. He is the most amazing person I know. I love him with all my heart.

Follow your dreams Forrest, you are truly unstoppable.

"The greatest weapon against stress is our ability to choose one thought over another."
— William James, Psychologist, Professor and Author

David Fawcett
Investigating Officer at the accident

My name is David Fawcett and I recently retired after 37 years as an Operational Police Officer. For the last 15 years of my career, I was an Ontario Provincial Police Constable, assigned to general uniform duties at the Southern Georgian Bay Detachment.

A good mutual friend of ours first introduced me to Forrest Willett back in 2000: Bob Hicks. I was impressed by Forrest's integrity and business savvy. I perceived him to be a friendly, sincere individual. A family man whose heart was in the right place. In my job you learn to read people.

On October 6, 2002, I was on duty in a marked police car. I received the radio call concerning a single vehicle crash in a field off Reeves Road in the Township of Tay. We had witness' information that persons were trapped inside the wreck. I rushed to the scene to find fire fighters and paramedics feverishly working to remove two men from the crushed car. Both men were unconscious and covered in blood. They appeared to be very seriously injured. I couldn't recognize Forrest and suspected he was present only because the car came back registered to him. I didn't know the other man who had been driving. It took a full 30 minutes to free them from the wreckage and they were quickly transported to hospital by ambulance. I have to state that we are extremely fortunate in this area to have skilled, dedicated paramedics and fire department personnel.

I interviewed several witnesses at the scene. One man who had been travelling north bound towards the involved vehicle stated he first saw it as it passed over some trees and was just beginning to roll sideways. The car was a large BMW sedan and must have been travelling at an extreme speed to become airborne. It's a testament to the strength of the design and construction of the vehicle that although crushed, it remained relatively intact after the impact with the ground. The car impacted the ground and bounced about 25 feet from a grazing cow.

From the scene, I attended the hospital. I was not able to interview either of the injured men. Treatment and care were the priority and I know never to get between a doctor or nurse and their patient. I spoke to the driver's son at the hospital, and he said that his father had called him from his cell phone stating that he would be late because he was test driving someone's vehicle. As he was speaking to his father the cell phone went dead.

I determined that family members had been notified and there wasn't anything else I could do to assist at that time. I subsequently completed and filed the appropriate reports. I later heard that Forrest and the driver were both slowly recovering from their serious injuries.

I often follow up on Forrest's amazing recovery. His very serious head injury would seem daunting and impossible to overcome to most people. But Forrest isn't most people. I am awed by his recovery and the hard work he continues to put toward regaining full function.

For all outward appearances he is his old self, still friendly and personable, a good man. I am very happy for him and his family.

I am happy to call him a friend.

"Be more concerned with your character than your reputation, because your character is what you really are, while your reputation is merely what others think you are."
— John Wooden, American Basketball Coach

Christine MacPherson
Speech-Language Pathologist

 I remember the first time I met Forrest with incredible clarity. It was a short time after his brain injury, he had just returned home, and he seemed fragile, passive and very scared.

He was in a lot of physical and emotional pain and was confused. As a speech-language pathologist (SLP) I had been asked to meet with Forrest to assess his "cognitive-communication" abilities and to develop a plan for therapy. He wasn't sure why a "speech therapist" was there to meet with him.

Despite this uncertainty, Forrest trusted what I had to say and stuck with me, and over a number of years, he worked harder than I could ever imagine. From that first introduction we slowly and surely developed a wonderful therapeutic relationship.

Today, many years after we stopped working together in our therapist-client relationship, I am proud to say that Forrest is my friend. I am also proud of Forrest for writing this incredibly valuable book.

This book not only tells his own story but offers hope and practical strategies to survivors and their families. Forrest has "walked the walk" and he delivers his clear, functional messages with a delicate balance between humor and compassion. He doesn't sugar coat his journey, and makes it crystal clear that rehabilitation can be a long, hard road. His message is: "I never said it was going to be easy, but it is going to be worth it!"

As a therapist who has been working in the field for over 25 years I know that rehabilitation, by its very nature, can create a situation where an individual is placed in a passive role. This passive role is necessary in the very early stages of recovery where a person's life hangs in the balance and we need to literally hand over a life to the medical experts.

As time passes, and rehabilitation begins, too often this passive role is perpetuated by well meaning therapists, doctors, friends and family members. It is so important to hand back "power" to people who have sustained a brain injury by providing choices, being respectful of decisions and truly collaborating in all aspects of every day life, big and little.

Through this book, Forrest has truly reclaimed his "power" and is sharing his incredible story with others. He motivates others to reclaim their own power.

Enjoy this wonderful story of resilience, compassion, inspiration and kindness. Enjoy the frankness, warts and all.

Enjoy the funny stories - Forrest can make you laugh, when others would cry. It's all a matter of perspective.

Thank you Forrest for teaching me what it means to not only survive, but to thrive.

Forrest, thank you for teaching all of us how to live, not just exist, after tragedy.

"To live is the rarest thing in the world. Most people exist, that is all."
— Oscar Wilde

Gary Warman
Occupational Therapist

 As a therapist there have been many people that I have had the pleasure of working with.

Many have stood out for their abilities or the severity of their injuries or illnesses. Others have stood out for their determination to improve or overcome their losses. Forrest is one of the latter.

I remember the first meeting with Forrest. The look in his eyes reminded me of a deer that had been caught in the headlights of a car. He appeared scared and was not sure what to do or how to respond. Due to injuries caused by the car accident he had gone from a busy and successful businessman to needing somebody with him all of the time to keep him safe from his own actions.

Forrest worked through many frustrations; feeling that nobody understood what he was going through, realizing that he was not safe to be left alone with his son, criticism from friends for embarrassing things that he did due to a loss of inhibitions, further injuries he sustained due to difficulty recognizing dangerous situations, loss of self-worth due to changes in his business and family life as well as the inability to do what he felt he needed to do. These all led to a change in life's focus and reorganizing his life and focusing on things that he could do in spite of his injuries and limitations.

As Forrest worked through his limitations, he was able to change priorities and move towards helping other people. He has been able to provide support for survivor's with similar injuries and provide encouragement to those who are struggling with their difficulties.

Forrest's will and determination to get better has been an inspiration for me. I have frequently used parts of his story to inspire people that are struggling to overcome their own limitations.

Claudia Maurice
Occupational Therapist

 I have had the privilege of working with Forrest, supporting him from an Occupational Therapy Rehabilitative perspective soon after his serious motor vehicle accident that on October 6, 2002.

Although I was not his initial treating therapist, I came to know Forrest during those difficult months that followed the accident. It has been a privilege to work with Forrest because since day one, he was an individual who put forth his best effort to regain some semblance of normalcy in his life, even during those periods when he felt overwhelmed and confused. Forrest's strength and determination to re-define himself as an individual and to gradually gain acceptance of the changes that have been imposed on him, has always impressed me.

The amount of times he has been knocked down in life and continues to get up is awe-inspiring.

In many ways, Forrest resembled a butterfly that is eventually able to break through its cocoon and eventually spread its wings and fly. Forrest initially presented as an individual who was withdrawn and really struggled to accept his changes. In many respects, Forrest did not even understand what his limitations were, which resulted in him experiencing many challenges.

Over the course of time, however, and a result of his strong conviction, motivation, determination, and sense of humor, as well as his acceptance of the necessary support to assist him to move forward with his life, he has been able to redefine the "new" Forrest. It has been my privilege to support Forrest through his lengthy, and at times difficult rehabilitative process. He has definitely been able to spread his wings and is now flying, sometimes even soaring forward. There is definitely no stopping him now!

As health care professionals, we can only assume to understand what it is truly like to have to struggle to cope with the traumatic effects of a brain injury and to forge ahead to redefine the new person that emerges following such a traumatic and devastating event. What I have learned over the years, however, is that such individuals have remarkable resiliency and the ability to move forward to lead productive and meaningful lives.

Although they may have an altered life path, they are able to evolve into remarkable individuals who demonstrate strength, courage, and at times a wonderful sense of humor. It never ceases to amaze me, in regards to how much I continue to learn from my clients. I have also come to realize that the key to working with individuals who have suffered life-changing events, is essentially to listen to them and "never say never" with respect to their abilities to achieve what is truly meaningful and important to them.

Forrest has taught me that no matter how high that mountain may seem, maintaining a positive attitude, sense of humor, strong conviction, level of dedication, and willingness to work with those that are there to assist them, can result in assuming a new purpose in life, as well as a sense of productivity, meaning and overall fulfillment. Life has many curves that at times can be painful to negotiate. With the right attitude, however, and a willingness to work hard, these curves can lead to an amazing path of recovery.

Thank you, Forrest, for the opportunity to be part of your journey. I know that you will only continue to spread your wings and fly, and capture the hearts of other as you have done with mine.

"Take chances, make mistakes. That's how you grow. Pain nourishes your courage. You have to fail in order to practice being brave"
— Mary Tyler Moore, Actress

Bob Hicks
Long time friend

My name is Bob Hicks. I have known Forrest for approximately 25 years and happy to call him a friend. Forrest and I first met through a business associate. He was relatively young but had already established a very good reputation with his clients and community. He was involved in many charities and fundraisers.

I knew Forrest before he was married and he was always popular and respected. Everything that Forrest attempted seemed to turn out golden. A common quote heard when talking about him was "Everything he touches turns to gold". There were some stresses but it never showed.

Forrest developed a business with franchises across Ontario, and they were thriving and growing by leaps and bounds. And then came that day....

I heard the stories from law enforcement friends and firemen. The stories were horrific and in the hospital the appearance of a young man that I knew very well was unrecognizable. I was sure that "IF" he recovered things would never ever be even half way normal again.

I have to give credit to his wife Julie as she stuck by his side through the very difficult times to follow, and I am sure that most women faced with a seemingly hopeless future with her husband would have taken the easy route and left. And most people would not have blamed her, but she persevered. Also to be raising their son and her "new child" Forrest because with his brain injury, he was almost child like as well. She truly has shown that a supportive wife is a true blessing to his ongoing recovery.

I know first hand how hard recovery is. My son has an acquired brain injury that we have been dealing with for years and we know about the simple, frustrating things such as memory loss, fatigue, and low drive. I am glad to have Forrest as a resource and friend to my son Joel as they can speak and talk about their frustrations together.

And now if you meet Forrest or my son, it would take a lot of scrutiny to find or see a problem, but they are dealing with issues of memory loss and the feeling of "What am I forgetting?" as well as other issues every second of the day.

I have to say there is only one thing that Forrest continues to work on very hard with no improvement and I can see how frustrated he gets, and that is his golf game.

Forrest is now back driving, working and golfing (although not very well) and recovering from a brain injury that people told him would be the end of a productive life.

Please share this book with someone you know in this position, as Forrest is living proof you can come back from a brain injury and depression. He is a great inspiration to everyone that know's his story, including my son and our entire family. I know complete recovery will take years, if ever, but where you are now from where you came is a Miracle.

I am proud that you call me your friend.

63309589R00110

Made in the USA
Lexington, KY
03 May 2017